Further Up
&
Further In

Understanding C. S. Lewis's
The Lion, the Witch and the Wardrobe

Further Up
&
Further In

BRUCE EDWARDS

BROADMAN
&HOLMAN
PUBLISHERS

NASHVILLE, TENNESSEE

Ten-Digit ISBN:0–8054–4070–4
Thirteen-Digit ISBN: 978–0–8054–4070–6

Published by Broadman & Holman Publishers
Nashville, Tennessee

Dewey Decimal Classification: 813
Subject Heading: LEWIS, C. S. CHRONICLES OF NARNIA \
BRITISH NOVELISTS

1 2 3 4 5 6 7 8 9 10   10 09 08 07 06 05

Contents

Dedication

This work is dedicated to my dear children: Matthew, Mary Elizabeth, Justin, Michael, Tracey, and Casey.

The wonder of childhood and the delights of fatherhood are ever before me because of you. Over many nights and over so many seasons I have watched you play "in the fields of the Lord," whether baseball, tennis, or basketball, on stage or in movies, creating songs of joy for CDs, and honoring God by your steadfastly clinging to him. His goodness is always reflected in your now adult faith, hope, and love for me. You keep me young in spirit and hopeful of heart.

Your lives have helped me to go *further up and further into* the Master's kingdom. May Narnia continue to live in your hearts as you bequeath its mysteries to your children and to theirs.

Through the Wardrobe: Our Passport to Narnia

I hope you're not the kind of reader who always skips the preface, because this one is really important. I know you expect all authors to say that, but in this case it really is true. To understand the kind of book I have written and how to get the most out of it, you really need to make it all the way through the preface. Just pretend it is called "chapter 1." Your adventure in Narnia really does start here, and it begins with my clever explanation of my book's title.

If you're puzzled by the title of this book about *The Lion, the Witch and the Wardrobe*, it is either because you have already read all The Chronicles—or you haven't. Sound paradoxical? If you have read them, you know that the title phrase comes *not* from this volume but rather from the last tale of The Chronicles, *The Last Battle;* if you haven't read *The Last Battle*, then you need some explanation of the phrase. And thereafter both sets of my readers deserve a defense of its use here.

In *The Last Battle*—no worries, there are no real spoilers ahead for those who may not have gotten to it yet—the Sons of Adam and Daughters of Eve make some surprising discoveries about the future of Narnia and their place in it. It seems only fitting that I draw my title from Mr. Tumnus, an alumnus, pardon the pun, of the White Witch's wintry, stony grip, rescued by Aslan, who explains near the climax of

The Last Battle that, in the end, all the faithful followers of Aslan get to go "further up and further in."

What does this mean? That they are privileged to fathom the true meaning of their lives and embrace the depth, height, and width of his great love for us. There is no end to Narnia, for it is "larger on the inside than it is on the outside," and there is no end to the surprise of joy and the glory of living in righteousness forever and ever in Aslan's presence. It is a picture, in other words, of our entry into eternity where we may by grace hear the words, "Well done, my good and faithful servant, enter into the joy of your Master."

That is what our goal is on both sides of the wardrobe: to go "further up and further in," to discover and remain in Aslan's presence, following his lead, completing the missions he sets for us, and gaining glorious comrades along the way to share grand adventures in the Spirit. We want to know what it means to be a Narnian, so we can learn better how to be a Son of Adam or a Daughter of Eve. But how, you ask, might we go "further up and further in" *The Lion, the Witch and the Wardrobe?*

Starting *in Medias Res*: Our Passport to Narnia

Let's start by explaining a bit why we are starting *here*, in *The Lion, the Witch and the Wardrobe*, rather than *somewhere else*. Who wants to know the end of the story before the beginning? Where's the suspense, the surprise, the climax in that? When we first enter Narnia, our passport is "through the wardrobe," and if we are getting there at all, we are getting there *in medias res*—"in the middle of things." We don't know what or where Narnia is, or what has happened to bring about its dreadful circumstances ("always winter and never Christmas"). We must read to find out. We have to pursue the text further up and further in to discover "the context" and the "chronology."

That is precisely the way the Pevensie children, with the help of Professor Kirke, must proceed. But isn't that the way we enter our world, too? We don't get to choose our parents or our continent or our fingerprints—and certainly not the stories that preceded us or any of the stories that may come after. We must learn as we go, guided by generous and helpful counselors.

Every human life is itself a story, a walking history. We are just inserted into the dialogue and flow of life that God has chosen. Thank goodness! For imagine our being invested with the decision of when and how to enter history, under what conditions, speaking what language, or perhaps none at all? (Think of the Father preparing his Son for his incarnate entry into our world.) Ah, the plot thickens! We are not wise enough, nor are we courageous enough to do that. Who could say for sure she is equipped and "ready" to enter this world when and where she pleases? But you see, the same is true of our entry into all human stories.

Think about it. Of course, we eventually want to learn about our origins, the day we were born, how illustrious our ancestors were, what clever things we said when we were young. And who hasn't longed to sit at his grandparents' side or mother's knee and hear again the story of some poignant episode from childhood? Yes, we want to know where we came from and what happened before we got here. But we may not want or need to know all of that before we can get on with our unfolding story in the present. It is usually when something happens in our lives that begs the question about what happened before. "Mommy, what was it like in our house before I came?"

C. S. Lewis felt the same way. His favorite stories as a child just had him jumping into the fray, entering where he could and as he could. Ignoring the "back story" at the start lest it obscure the story before him, Lewis loved to enter the world without a precise map so he could discover things for himself. The reason this is important, if you have not guessed by now, is that once upon a time *The Lion, the Witch and the Wardrobe* was the first of the stories to be written and published and was the Narnian tale most readers started with from 1950 until the 1980s. But now *The Magician's Nephew* is listed first in the current publisher's order, followed by *The Lion, the Witch and the Wardrobe*. This change was made presumably so that new readers would have to start their safari into Narnia at its "beginning," thus prescribing a "chronological reordering."

I beg to differ. as do, thankfully, the makers of the recent Narnian movie series, who wisely set out themselves to start with *The Lion.* They too wish to have us enter Narnia through the wardrobe first—rather than through the use of, say, "magic rings," the means by which one particular Son of Adam and Daughter of Eve go to and fro in *The Magician's Nephew.* (Hmmmm. Sound like any other famous fairy tale you may have recently read or seen a movie about?) The truth is, we do not really have reasons to care about the origins of Narnia (which are, indeed, revealed in *The Magician's Nephew*) until we have first been there to discover for ourselves what has happened; and then we will find ourselves curious about how things got that way, hungry for history, and, perhaps, chronology.

Quite honestly, the way in which the rest of the Narnian tales unfold and what they demand and forecast in terms of dramatic impact and progression of plot are honored best by starting with the story of Aslan's redemption of Narnia and his defeat of the White Witch. (The true parallel here, in my mind, is between the Old and New Testaments; when we wish to introduce someone to "the way, the truth, and the life," do we start with the Gospels or with Genesis? Eventually, we will get to Beginnings, but the story of Jesus is the real motivation to read the story of Genesis; his "new" story in the Gospels validates and fulfills the "old" story in obvious historical and literary ways.)

There are some neat surprises and not a few ironies revealed in *The Magician's Nephew* that are, in fact, "spoiled" if we do not read *The Lion, the Witch and the Wardrobe* first. I won't tell you what those are, but those who have read them both know what I mean. Now there may be good reasons to *study* Narnia in a certain order, the way some literary critics do, but to *read* them in chronological order the first time we encounter them? By no means.

To me, and the vast majority of Chronicles readers I have met or taught, the best way to enter Narnia will always be through the wardrobe, that is, through the order in which they were drafted and published by Lewis. In this order the progressive revelation of Aslan's character and Narnian history are best encountered. Narnia did not begin with Lewis creating a tight outline of its history and a detailed catalog of key "personnel" who would inhabit this landscape, coupled with the marshaling of voluminous historical data or a geographically exhaustive series of maps (the way, for instance, Lewis's friend J. R. R. Tolkien apparently invented Middle-Earth).

I am aware that Lewis once exchanged letters with a little boy named Laurence, who proposed, against his mother's protestations, reading The Chronicles in "chronological order," that is, following the order of events as sequenced in "Narnian time." This would mean reading The Chronicles in this order: *The Magician's Nephew*, then *The Lion, the Witch and the Wardrobe, The Horse and His Boy, Prince Caspian, The Voyage of the Dawn Treader, The Silver Chair*, and *The Last Battle*. But Lewis's apparent endorsement of his young correspondent's entreaty is to me just an example of his graciousness and desire to reward the earnestness (and precociousness) of a young reader who probably reminded him just a little of himself. In that same letter Lewis confesses, "So perhaps it does not matter very much in what order anyone reads them. I'm not even sure that all the others were written in the same order in which they were published. I never keep notes of that sort of thing and never remember dates."[1] There is, for me, a certain fitness and propriety in proceeding with the narrative order that first led Lewis into Narnia himself: an unexpected and unannounced encounter with Aslan, which we will explore in the first chapter. And that means starting with *The Lion, the Witch and the Wardrobe*.

How *Further Up and Further In* Tries to Be Different: An Inside-out Approach

I wanted in writing *Further Up and Further In* to provide both novice and experienced readers something that will increase their enjoyment every time they come to *The Lion, the Witch and the Wardrobe* (or the movie made of it). *Further Up and Further In* won't explore every possible detail you may want to know about Narnia because that is not its design, and there is plenty to be discovered that this small volume could not possibly include. I had no incentive to provide encyclopedic coverage of each jot and tittle because Paul Ford's wonderful volume *Companion to Narnia* (cited later in "For Further Reading") already does that.

The truth is, literary encyclopedias provide a specific service and are useful particularly after we have put the book down. They represent an "outside-in" approach—forging facts and compiling connections exterior to the text and using them to interpret and elucidate what you have already read long after you have left the intimate setting of the book itself. They draw you naturally outside the world the tale has created; they occupy you with things and ideas and people the book points to and try to answer nagging questions you may have. And then, at their best, like Ford's *Companion to Narnia,* they will send you back to the text for more interaction with Aslan and his creation. But at their worst—and I am afraid this is what most encyclopedias do—they may take you "further out and further away" and, in this case, force you to remain an outsider to the continuing experience of Narnia. (One can become an "expert" on Narnia, so to speak, without ever living there. What a pity!)

A large part of what makes Narnia terrific, engrossing, and life-changing is its ability not only to deliver a world that is strange and compelling but also to make *our own world* strange and compelling as well. Its genius, if you will, is its ability to make us long for a world like Aslan's and then to help us discover in ours the evidence that Aslan has been here too, and to motivate us to uncover the implications of that visit. A Narnian sojourn makes us dissatisfied with our world for all the right reasons and then points us to a pathway to our true home and our true identity. Indeed, that is what any reading of The Chronicles ought to evince and maybe even what a book about *The Lion, the Witch and the Wardrobe* should do as well!

That indeed is my challenge in *Further Up and Further In.* I am attempting what I call an "inside-out" approach, designed to increase your appreciation for the strangeness and oddness of what is going on inside Aslan's story on several levels while we are inside Narnia, not outside of it. I don't want you to spend a minute more outside the text than you have to because our time in Narnia is too precious to waste in search of external sources. The Chronicles tell a simple story on the surface but one that is actually clever and complex and thus one that repays many visits and rereadings. At the same time, because of those very revisits, our experiences threaten to become commonplace and ordinary. My job is to help you keep coming back to Narnia and finding it as exhilarating and as disarmingly fresh as the first time you visited it. A tall order, yes, but one worth the risk. Fortunately, Lewis has written just the sort of work that enables us to enjoy that freshness every time!

This is what I call an "indigenous" approach to Narnia, and I derive it primarily from recommendations that Lewis himself makes in *An Experiment in Criticism* (Cambridge: Cambridge UP, 1961), his most extended statement about good reading and what it consists of, as well as its enduring value. In this book, whose title belies its actual vitality and poignancy, Lewis argues that modern readers are often handicapped by would-be critics and so-called "helpful" reviewers who end up reducing great works to matters of mere taste ("read this and you will show how 'contemporary' your thinking is"), mere paraphrase ("all this book really means is . . ."), or mere form ("yes, the themes and characters here are ghastly, but notice how beautifully written the work is"). The peril of such stilted forms of reading is that it can turn readers into *users* rather than *receivers* of the words and worlds offered to them by writers. And for Lewis this is the worst possible destiny for an author or his work.

Users of texts reduce the meaning and impact of the works to what they can successfully paraphrase and what already fits into their preexisting worldview. In other words, they read down to their current level of insight and being—making a book say what they want it to say, delivering only the experiences they wish to repeat, closing themselves off to anything new, challenging, or different. Receivers of texts, by contrast, willingly enter the worlds of their author and reside there with respect, curiosity, and anticipation. They take the risk of reading things they may disagree with or not understand completely but do so wisely, not naïvely; they are open to discovery and to wrestling with novel circumstances. Here is Lewis's comely way of expressing this in another of his volumes:

> One man carries his Englishry abroad with him and brings it home unchanged. Wherever he goes he consorts with the other English tourists. By a good hotel he means one that is like an English hotel. He complains of

the bad tea where he might have had excellent coffee. But there is another sort of traveling and another sort of reading. You can eat the local food and drink the local wines, you can share the foreign life, you can begin to see the foreign country as it looks, not to the tourist, but to its inhabitants. You can come home modified, thinking and feeling as you did not think and feel before. . . .

I should hope to choose this second way of traveling and reading, for I will then be led by it to newer and fresher enjoyments, things I could never have met . . . modes of feeling, flavours, atmospheres, nowhere accessible. . . . I have lived nearly sixty years with myself and my own century and am not so enamoured of either as to desire no glimpse of a world beyond them.[2]

This is the way we too wish to traverse Narnia, as receivers, eyes and ears open, trying not to import too many of our own tried-and-true, and therefore, "orchestrated" experiences but rather desiring a *"glimpse of a world beyond them."* (Please note that this is not a liberal versus conservative posture, for readers of various convictions and alignments can be caught in the trap of using texts and thus blunting their impact. Anyone who has ever proof texted a Bible verse to "prove" an improbable point is a user, no matter how salutary his overall convictions may be.)

Lewis thus taught his students that a text is both something *said* (*logos*) and something *made* (*poiema*). An author fashions a world (and thereby reveals a worldview) in whatever he writes and offers the reader an open invitation to inhabit that world—to become incarnate within it for as long as she finds it interesting, challenging, engaging. (No reader, by the way, is ever under obligation to stay with a text that is actually injurious or just plain confusing to her. This is spiritual discernment, not "using" texts in Lewis's "abusive" sense.) The role of the reader is thus clearly complementary to the role of the writer.

The reader agrees to enter a new landscape and is therein asked by the writer to leave behind her prejudices, expectations, and preferences, all the while trying to see, feel, hear, touch, and taste the world the author has invented. The author's *logos* (message) and *poiema* (literary form) contribute to the enjoyment and the education of the reader—but only if the reader is not attempting to circumvent the reader process by "using" the text for her own purposes but rather endeavors to "receive" the text on its own merits.

According to Lewis, any book that is reducible to either a paraphrase of its message or a simple tracing of its form is not a work worthy of the reader's ongoing attention. What he loved in literature, and what he hoped to produce in Narnia, is a tale whose form and whose message were united and inseparable—an "incarnate" word—whose pleasure and whose meaning had to be experienced together or not at all. Long before Marshall McLuhan said it famously, Lewis knew that "the medium is the message," and vice versa.

Finding Our Way into Narnia

But, you ask, "So what?" I admit Lewis's argument is intricate and multifaceted, and I am close to oversimplifying it here, something neither practical nor fair to him. Let me just summarize its relevance for *Further Up and Further In* by saying: Lewis believed we should read actively so we could "transcend" ourselves and "enlarge our being" by encountering new worlds and fresh perspectives as we travel expectantly within an author's landscape. My job, following Lewis's tenets, is thus to keep you *inside* Narnia, inside the wardrobe so to speak, as long as possible, choosing the right moments to remind, illustrate, compel you to look again through the eyes of the Pevensie children and the other Narnians in the tale through both direct commentary and intriguing sidebars.

We shall simply see what we find as we travel together, trying neither to race ahead nor to preclude your own unique discoveries. My comments through the *Further Up and Further In's* six chapters are offered to highlight and intimate rather than inhibit or obscure the Narnian worldview. Along the way this also means, inevitably, that I may need to allude to and/or carefully examine settings, characters, circumstances, and outcomes that explain why *The Lion, the Witch and the Wardrobe* might indeed remind us of *a certain other story* that took place in our world—and the difference that should make to us.

Further Up and Further In is designed in the end to be a companion rather than an intruder in your enjoyment of the work. It tries to walk beside you without spoiling the view. You know the difference, right? A wily companion says, "Wow, did you notice that beautiful tree back there? Want to take a closer look?" The intruder says, "Stop this instant! We must go back and video that tree, take a specimen home, and Google it when we get to my laptop so we can verify each and every one of its features." The companion says, "Yes, let's stay a while and ponder"; the intruder says, "Let's take this out of its natural context and put it under the microscope." To put it another way, using another of Lewis's useful metaphors, we want to "look *along*" Narnia, as well as "look *at*" it." We're not just gathering "data"; we're participating in an adventure too![3]

My plan for an inside-out, indigenous trek into Narnia is different from this intruder mentality. There are seventeen chapters in *The Lion, the Witch and the Wardrobe* (LWW), seventeen precisely paced and elegantly plotted chapters that, to me, fall into five distinct groupings by which I will guide your reflections on your reading:

Chapters 1–3 of LWW ("Finding What You're Not Looking For") introduce us to the Pevensies and to the professor and prepare us for what lies just beyond the wardrobe door through the fur coats. Chapters 4–6 of LWW ("Turkish Delights and Other Tempting Confections") reveal the heart of darkness lurking in each of us and what has happened to one particular being who has completely given herself over to evil. Chapters 7–9 of LWW ("Hospitality Is as Hospitality Does") teach us about what hospitality and friendship really entail and why the wickedness dominating Narnia cannot endure as long as faithful friends pursue righteousness. Chapters 10–13 of LWW ("Aslan on the Move") demonstrate what happens when Aslan is on the move and why we can and must trust him. Chapters 14–17 of LWW ("Deep Magic Is Never Enough") inform us about why Deep Magic can only tell us when we have gone wrong and can't of itself right that wrong. The climax and aftermath accentuate the mighty power of Aslan and the deeper magic that redeems and surpasses the knowledge from the dawn of time.

For each thematic grouping I have thus written my own chapter containing a companion overview and relevant commentary that will highlight the flow of the narrative in these groupings with an eye on what's happening and the significance of what we see and hear. As appropriate, toward the end of each chapter, I also gently identify some emerging themes and a few character traits, and then notice a few personal discoveries that the children and the full-time Narnian residents make along the way. And, oh, yes, occasionally I have provided some "outside" information as unobtrusively as possible, a kind of working glossary of key terms that may add to your enjoyment. At the end of the book, I have also compiled some useful discussion questions to guide a group or personal study of this exciting tale.

Here come my six chapters. I start in chapter 1 with a focused introduction to the life and work of C. S. Lewis and his love of fairy tales and the reason that is important. Such a compact chapter cannot at all do justice to the marvel of his range of endeavor, incredible fruitfulness, and continuing impact. But who he is and what he did are in some ways not as important as what and why he wrote, and he would be the first to tell us this.

Since I am the one writing *this* book, and you have been so kind as to accept my plea to read this preface and have indeed made it to its last paragraph, let me be the first to tell you this about him.

Acknowledgments

I f a writer is honest, he will confess that his book really has many "authors"—or at least countless unnamed and unnameable influences, some direct, some indirect, some ridiculous, some sublime, and some completely nonliterary. I must acknowledge a semblance of them here.

Over the years my understanding of Narnia has been shaped by many friends and readers of C. S. Lewis, none more profoundly than my wife, Joan, who introduced me to The Chronicles soon after we were married. I had already been enamored of Lewis but not of his fiction as such. But Joan has an intuitive sense of what's important and lasting in a book or a life and more than thirty years ago shared her insights with me. For this I will always be indebted to her first. Sweetie, thank you for many hours of quiet walks and deep, reflective conversation on what's real.

Though it may seem odd, a significant portion of this book was written while I was in Tunis, Tunisia, North Africa, directing the computer training aspects of a U. S. State Department Middle East Partnership Initiative Grant designed to train Tunisian journalism students in what it means to serve their readers under a democratic, free-press regime. At the same time I was away in Tunis, my wife, Joan, was serving in a relief and training mission herself in Rwanda and Burundi, East Africa, equipping widows and abandoned mothers and children in how to sew and weave and earn a living for their families. Somehow reflecting on Joan's servant heart and willingness to take risky journeys and my experience of the earnest and eager efforts of my students in Tunisia have been a real inspiration to me to see Narnia afresh, as we were both "strangers in a strange land," just as

Peter, Susan, Lucy, and Edmund were when they went through the wardrobe the first time. That strangeness is compelling and hard to preserve, but it is worth preserving.

No one has taught me more how about to read Clive Staples Lewis than Lewis himself, and I urge anyone who has come to Professor Lewis through the reading of *The Lion, the Witch and the Wardrobe* immediately to stop what she or he is doing and read everything else (I mean everything) Lewis has written on all topics. This is the best preparation for truly understanding and appreciating Narnia for all that it is worth.

Of course, that could be impractical. So let me point the reader especially to Lewis's *Surprised by Joy,* which provides unwitting but poignant commentary on the underlying themes of The Chronicles; because he has already lived their lives in some fashion, he can provide expert testimony to "reasons for the hope that is in" the Pevensie children during their sojourn in Narnia. The "For Further Reading" bibliography following chapter 6 of this book provides some immediately helpful guidance for those who want more traditional secondary sources for advanced study. There you will find the names of those people most to be entrusted with the Lewis legacy: Lindskoog, Dorsett, Downing, Duriez, Root, Schakel, Hooper, Hinten, King, Ford, Carnell, and Kreeft. Each of these writers—some of whom I count as friends and fellow scholars and some of whom I regard as pedestal-dwelling giants (you decide who you are!)—contributes much to our understanding of who Lewis is, how Narnia came to be, and why we should rejoice. These writers all exemplify what Lewis said about the New Testament writers in his essay on "Christianity and Literature": "They cared not about Genius, but about Goodness." Their genius comes through anyway.

I offer my ever-growing thanks to Matt Jacobson, my agent at Loyal Arts, whose sage advice steered me toward the steady hands (and eyes) of the great folks at Broadman & Holman. (Matt understands the sheer lunacy/challenge of writing two books simultaneously on Narnia without slavish overlap or redundancy.) To Leonard G. Goss and the talented editorial, creative, and marketing staff at Broadman & Holman including John Landers, Kim Overcash, Courtney Brooks, Jeff Godby, David Schrader, Paul Mikos, Robin Patterson, Heather Hulse, and David Chandler: my earnest gratitude and awed respect for their design, copy editing, and promotional expertise.

Many friends over time have taught me much about what and how and why to read, and I want to mention some of them here just to let them know that I realize my indebtedness and that I hope to repay them by writing this volume about something and someone we mutually care a great deal about: Scott and Garilyn Calhoun; Tom and Alice Cook; Bill and Margie Larson; Tom and Pat Sanford; Michael and Jill Malanga; Mark and Gemma Eberle; Barbara and George Toth; Robert and Rachel Ochieng; Purity Kiambi; Mary and Humphrey Muchiri; Lyle Dorsett; David and Dana Abdo; and Japanese Inklings scholar, Ms. Kyoko Yuasa. Thanks also to Alice Cook, who prepared the index.

I also owe a special thanks to my supervisors and colleagues at Bowling Green State University, who have allowed me the breadth (and breath) to pursue this publishing project in the midst of my duties as associate dean of Distance Education and International Programs. I must thank sincerely executive vice president Linda Dobb and associate vice president and dean of continuing education William K. Balzer for their encouragement to work on my passion for Lewis Studies while cautioning me in their own distinctive way that all work and no play may be detrimental to my health! To Dr. Marcia Salazar-Valentine: my sincere thanksgiving for your continuing friendship and shining example as a fellow administrator; Marcia, write that book on Jane Austen!

At the same time, my two creative staffs, one at IDEAL (*Interactive Distance Education for All Learners*) and one at the Center for International Programs, have by their innovation and industriousness allowed me to steal some time "late in the day" to complete this project. Terry Herman, the former director, and Connie Molnar, current director of IDEAL, make working at BGSU's continuing education unit a rewarding, reassuring, and peaceful place to call home each weekday. The same goes for my colaborers in international education—Jeff Grilliot, Anne Saviers, Diane Regan, Yolanda Patton, Sally Raymont, Nicole Myers, and Kathy Beattie.

And so to you, dear reader, as fellow explorer, I commend and thank you for your investment of time and interest in this little work of love and companionship. It is good to be in your company, to read The Chronicles alongside such a willing and winsome traveler, and to find together the lamppost that leads us forward into the light.

Chapter 1

Meeting C. S. Lewis:
Retelling the Gospel as a Fairy Tale

It is somewhat taken for granted today that Christians may write gripping, challenging, even best-selling fiction, including entries in the once-scorned genres of fantasy, science fiction, and fairy tales. But once upon a time, few Christians were actively engaged in writing for a popular or wide audience outside their communities of faith. Fewer still were able to integrate faith and worldview effectively in imaginative prose. The most illustrious twentieth-century pioneer in this frontier of faith, hands down, is C. S. Lewis, creator of The Chronicles of Narnia.

Besides the millions of copies that The Chronicles have sold annually since the 1950s, nearly all of Lewis's works remain in print, whether theological, literary, or imaginative—a remarkable fact and one true of few prolific authors living, let alone dead. But who's kidding whom? Hardly any writer, Christian or not, in the Western world is as prolific, well quoted, or quotable as Lewis. And in annual polls of clergy and laity registering the most influential Christian writers in their lives, Lewis consistently is at the top, and across a wide spectrum of communions, traditions, and denominations.

Born in Belfast, Northern Ireland, on November 29, 1898, Lewis served admirably in World War I, earned formidable academic credentials at Oxford University, became a world-renowned teacher and prolific literary historian and critic at both Oxford and Cambridge Universities, and led an amazingly productive career as a Christian apologist, memoirist, essayist, poet, and fantasist. His late-in-life, star-crossed marriage to American poet, Joy Davidman Gresham, was a *cause celebre* and the subject of a popular teleplay, stage play, and Hollywood movie, each entitled *Shadowlands*. He died quietly yet auspiciously on November 23, 1963, the same day U.S. President John F. Kennedy was assassinated.

This dispassionate, dictionary-like nutshell hardly conveys the momentous, astounding story of Lewis's life and its continuing impact on readers and believers around the world. To paraphrase the psalmist, "Who was Clive Staples Lewis that we should be mindful of him?"[1]

Separated by Grief, Surprised by Joy

If we know anything about who Lewis was before his conversion to Christ, we would know that he represents absolutely the least likely person slated to accept the gospel as truth, let alone become one of its greatest champions. But if we know anything about the Person to whom he surrendered in faith, nothing should surprise us, except, as Lewis put it in his spiritual autobiography, joy itself. In that volume, *Surprised by Joy* (New York: Harcourt, 1955), Lewis charts the story of his conversion, and we learn directly from this narrative the following, solemn, singular fact just a few chapters in: "C. S. Lewis, grand defender of Christianity, lost his faith when he was 9 years old in a profound and principled way." How's that as a good start for a would-be Christian fantasist or famous defender of the faith?

In this, his most personal and disclosive work, Lewis recounts how his mother Flora's illness and eventual death broke the tranquility and sanctity of the Lewis household when he was only nine and spends the rest of its pages documenting the sometimes melancholy but ultimately salutary search ostensibly for the lost security he had taken for granted during the peace and settledness of his early childhood. We sometimes find what we are not looking for. If we seek our lives, we shall lose them; if we lose ourselves in the search, we may find our true identity. The chief revelation of his life, Lewis intimates, is that there are indeed more important discoveries and possessions than security and settledness and that real life consists in knowing one's Creator.

Before his mother's passing, Lewis explains that he had had an idyllic youth, a life filled with three glorious things: books, imaginative play with brother Warren (whom he called "Warnie"), and an ephemeral but fulfilling taste of joy, the latter intimately connected to the first two. As he suggests, "My father's house was filled with books. . . . I am a product of long corridors, empty sunlit rooms, upstairs indoor silences, attics explored in solitude, distant noises of gurgling cisterns and pipes, and the noise of wind under the tile. Also, of endless books. . . . Nothing was forbidden me. In the seemingly endless rainy afternoons I took volume after volume from the shelves" (p. 10).

Throughout his young life, whether immersed in fiction like E. Nesbit's *The Amulet* or Beatrix Potter's *Peter Rabbit* or in poetry like Longfellow's *Saga of King Olaf*, the precocious Lewis was alert to something more than just mundane plot details or poetic imagery—an intangible, numinous feeling pointing him beyond the natural and into the eternal. Myth and fairy tale ruled his imagination and mediated this subtle but real transcendent touch. And imaginative play? His deep friendship with his brother Warnie, whose penchant for creating miniature playsets, like the toy garden he invented for their mutual pleasure, gave Lewis his first glimpse of a certain elusive feeling which he as a child associated with autumn. These were intimations of immortality, "'patches of Godlight' in the woods of our experience."[2]

The joy Lewis fleetingly possessed ended abruptly with his mother's death, which set in motion years of doubt, sadness, and, worst of all, alienation between Lewis and his father. It strained and stained the image of his father in him, mocking the notion of a benevolent heavenly Father. Lewis had prayed fervently for his mother to be healed, and when she was not, he was embittered toward God. More shockingly, Lewis had sought earnestly for his father to embrace him, to comfort him and brother Warnie in their

3

profound grief, but instead he withdrew, violently, from his fatherhood over the boys, and with him took all of their hope and exhausted all of their faith. What love was left for the boys was spent on their common plight and their uncommon brotherhood.

Of course, many children lose loved ones before reaching maturity; Lewis is not unique in that. But his mother's death in effect dealt him and his brother a double loss. Their father Albert simply never recovered from Flora's death; unable to cope with single parenting, he sent the boys off to a series of boarding schools whose darkness and bullying haunted the Lewis brothers most of the rest of their lives. (One school, in particular, Lewis depicts in great detail in a heartbreaking chapter called "Concentration Camp" in *Surprised by Joy*.) Lewis and Warnie spent much of their adult life perplexed and angry, trying to find a way to penetrate Albert's cocoon of hurt, devastation, and loneliness. Before his father's death, Lewis had indeed reconciled with and forgiven him but only by the supernatural love and grace found in his heavenly Father, whose consolation he experienced after coming to faith.[3]

Not Safe, but Good

From our temporal point of view, Lewis endured a tortured youth and survived a tumultuous adolescence. However, by heaven's logic, that Lewis underwent this trauma is the greatest gift he could have received, for it sent him on his lifelong pursuit of the Author of joy. This is not something the budding young fantasy writer and Christian apologist could wish for, nor would we think it healthy that he would. But it points out something about God that Lewis convincingly conveys in creating the great lion king, Aslan, in the first tale of the Narnian series: "he is not safe, but he is good."

If we were doing it, we'd write the script a bit differently, wouldn't we? We would carefully circumscribe our young artist's life so that he would be placed in a safe, quiet, Christian home where he could be nurtured throughout childhood in calm, peaceful surroundings without turmoil or trouble, memorizing the Scriptures colorfully arrayed on the always well-supplied refrigerator. His Sunday school-teaching parents would provide the security, the affirmation, the ongoing protection that would insulate him

4

from injury, doubt, or fear. He would be bathed from start to finish in the deep love, the tender care, the awesome wonder of a God who ever lives to keep us safe from hurt, so he could be perfectly poised to live a life without exposure to disappointment or psychological harm, ready ever to tell the answer for the hope within him. Answers at no real cost to him, they nevertheless would be offered in good faith to the world at large.

Or so we sometimes think the Christian life is supposed to be.

We know if we read the Bible or review the lives of the saints of old, or the saints of today, there is no costless grace, there are no unwounded pilgrims, and there remain no meaningful answers that are not hard won. What hope, what answers, what apologetics or wholesome fantasy writing could emerge from such an artificially controlled life? That is the lesson to be drawn not just from Lewis's life but from every servant described in the Bible and from your life and mine too. Lewis, like other servants of God, "learned obedience through suffering." If this were a safe world, the Son of God would never have left heaven. The abundant life he brought with him cost him his own.

Lewis's prodigious learning gave him the opportunity to build a stellar academic career so that he could pursue with a pure heart his real vocation of communicating the gospel in fresh and refreshing ways in multiple genres and for a diversity of audiences. Those who read deeply into Lewis's canon of work find there a wholesome and engaging mix of vibrant wit, theological sophistication, sage counsel, and arresting metaphor. Lewis always writes out of a profound gratitude to the God who sought him and saved him during his most hopeless circumstances. He also proceeds graciously and humbly, identifying with the lost and wayfaring, among whom he once was. He tells them what they need to hear but also how they need to hear it. It is also, one must add, what they desperately want to hear.

His poetry and his prose create an expectancy in readers that lifts their hearts, challenges their worldview, and reminds of landmark truths they may have forgotten or discarded. In all this Lewis regarded himself as the "unprofitable servant" in Jesus' parable, doing "only that which is his duty to do." He has been given a great gift, the grace and mercy of God, and it is only right that he should share it among those who long to hear good news from home, from their "true country." Since he has lived this journey himself, he can express this longing compellingly and convincingly as he does in this passage from his most widely read work of apologetics, *Mere Christianity*:

> If I find in myself a desire which no experience in this world can satisfy, the most probable explanation is that I was made for another world. If none of my earthly pleasures satisfy it that does not prove that the universe is a fraud. Probably earthly pleasures were never meant to satisfy it, but only to arouse it, to suggest the real thing. If that is so, I must take care, on the one hand, never to despise, or be unthankful for, these earthly blessings, and on the other, never to mistake them for the something else of which they are only a kind of copy, or echo, or mirage. I must keep alive in myself the desire for my true country, which I shall not find till after death; I must never let it get snowed under or turned aside; I must make it the main object of life to press on to that other country and to help others to do the same.[4]

Seeing with the Heart

As Lewis relates the story in *Surprised by Joy*, the one significant contribution his father did make to his journey to manhood was rescuing him from his last, harrowing boarding-school experience and placing him in the homeschool of his own former, now retired, tutor, William Kirkpatrick. Under the man he called "the Great Knock," Lewis was schooled in the art of Socratic dialogue, of applying rigorous reason and logic to understanding the world and its texts. Lewis acknowledges Kirkpatrick as the one who really teaches him how to think lucidly and to express himself with precision—with neither stilted exaggeration nor abject generalization.

But *Surprised by Joy* is frank in depicting Lewis's return to faith and equilibrium not primarily as a rationalistic process but essentially as a recovery of his imagination, which certainly sustained him through many dark nights of the soul through his continuing love of myth and fairy tale. At one point he refers to nineteenth-century Christian writer George MacDonald, whose fantastic adventure, *Phantastes,* served as a corrective work that Lewis claims, in a memorable phrasing, "baptized his imagination." It led Lewis to glimpse for the first time since childhood a pathway into the realm of the supernatural, something he later recognizes as "holiness."[5] His famous summary statement of his journey to faith captures well the impact of his recovery of vision:

> In reading Chesterton, as in reading MacDonald, I did not know what I was letting myself in for. A young man who wishes to remain a sound Atheist cannot be too careful of his reading. There are traps everywhere—"Bibles laid open, millions of surprises," as Herbert says, "fine nets and stratagems." God is, if I may say it, very unscrupulous.[6]

As his literary career evolved, Lewis wrote well-received works of science fiction, wise and sprightly volumes of Christian apologetics, and many learned tomes on medieval and renaissance literature, but his heart was always centered in myth and fairy tale. His greatest triumph and most enduring works were destined to be his Narnian tales, for they both redeem his lifelong struggles and recapture the true end of his search for joy. Indeed, the question most people want to ask C. S. Lewis after they read The Chronicles of Narnia is well expressed by a young reader, Meredith, who wrote to him three years before his death in 1963, asking, "What inspired your books?"

"Really I don't know. Does anyone know where exactly an idea comes from? With me all fiction begins with pictures in my head. But where the pictures come from I couldn't say."[7]

Ah, those pictures! When he explained the origins of Narnia, Lewis always pointed to these recurring images:

> All my seven Narnian books, and my three science-fiction books, began with seeing pictures in my head. At first they were not a story, just pictures. They all began with a picture of a Faun carrying an umbrella and parcels in a snowy wood. This picture had been in my mind since I was about sixteen. Then one day, when I was about forty, I said to myself: "Let's try to make a story about it."
>
> At first I had very little idea how the story would go. But then suddenly Aslan came bounding into it. I think I had been having a good many

dreams of lions about that time. Apart from that, I don't know where the Lion came from or why He came. But once He was there he pulled the whole story together, and soon He pulled the other six Narnian stories in after Him."[8]

It can't be put more simply or eloquently than that. Aslan pulled the stories together—and Lewis himself—into Narnia. And that is probably as good a description as any of what happens to us when we enter the wardrobe. *Aslan pulls us in, and we keep seeing pictures in our heads.* How intriguing to witness the intrepid Lucy and the irreverent Edmund stumbling into the chill and wonder of wintry Narnia, meeting up with such contrasting Narnian characters. How interesting that it is Mr. Tumnus, the faun with the umbrella and parcels, whom Lucy first sees, and that it is the wicked white witch who is waiting to greet Edmund. How different their respective reactions are to hearing that "Aslan is on the move"! But none of this should surprise us too much.

The emphasis in Lewis's fiction (and nonfiction) is always "seeing with the heart," of apprehending images and tracing metaphors that instill faith and inspire journeys into the never-never land of the Spirit. For the heart reveals our true character, and, ultimately, where our treasure is. And the perfect genre for hosting such stories and themes is the fairy tale. C. S. Lewis and J. R. R. Tolkien, now famous as the creator of Middle-Earth, both lived and taught at Oxford University from the mid-1920s through the early 1950s and, once acquainted, became fast friends. Over time the two medieval and Renaissance literature professors spent a lot of time together talking about mythology and storytelling—particularly the art of the fairy tale.

They learned they both had grown up devouring and inventing tales of fantastic adventure, and they realized that neither had ever met anyone quite like the other. Both "Jack" Lewis (as he was called by friends) and "Tollers" (as Tolkien was called by Jack) had more in common with each other than with any other friend or colleague they had ever known. In fact, one could say that they shared deep convictions about almost everything—except Christianity.[9]

When the two first met in 1926, Lewis had finally grown into an agnostic on the search, jettisoning his now waning adolescent atheism with vigor and curiosity; Tolkien was a stalwart Christian believer, raised as a devout Catholic, unshy about sharing his faith. If Lewis's conversion to Christ comes at the end of an arduous imaginative and intellectual journey, Tolkien is central to its climax. In a 1931 letter to childhood friend Arthur Greeves, Lewis credits Tolkien (and mutual friend Hugo Dyson) with helping him see that his love of myth and fairy tale had simultaneously blinded him to, yet prepared him for, the final acknowledgment that the Gospels tell the authentic, eyewitness story of a "true myth":

> Now what Dyson and Tolkien showed me was this: that if I met the idea of sacrifice in a Pagan story I didn't mind at all: again, that if I met the idea of god sacrificing himself to himself. . . . I liked it very much and was mysteriously moved by it: again, that the idea of the dying and reviving god (Balder, Adonis, Bacchus) similarly moved me provided I met it anywhere except in the Gospels. The reason was that in Pagan stories I was prepared to feel the myth as profound and suggestive of meaning beyond my grasp even tho' I could not say in cold prose "what it meant."
>
> Now the story of Christ is simply a true myth: a myth working on us in the same way as the others, but with this tremendous difference *that it really happened*: and one must be content to accept it in the same way, remembering that it is God's myth where the others are men's myths: i.e., the Pagan stories are God expressing Himself through the mind of poets, using such images as He found there, while Christianity is God expressing Himself through what we call "real things."[10]

Tolkien himself made explicit the connection between how fairy tales touch the soul and how the Gospel account of the incarnation embodies true history in a fascinating lecture called "On Fairy-Stories." This address provides keen insight into why the Narnian Chronicles resonate with Gospel-like familiarity in the story of Aslan's death and resurrection. One can imagine that Tolkien had shared some version of these thoughts during their fateful stroll on Addison's Walk the night Lewis made the transition from skeptic to theist:

> The Gospels contain a fairy-story, or a story of a larger kind which embraces all the essence of fairy-stories. They contain many marvels— peculiarly artistic,[11] beautiful, and moving: "mythical" in their perfect, self-contained significance; and at the same time powerfully symbolic and allegorical; and among the marvels, the greatest and most complete conceivable *eucatastrophe.*
>
> The Birth of Christ is the eucatastrophe of Man's history. The Resurrection is the eucatastrophe of the story of the Incarnation. This story begins and ends in joy. It has pre-eminently the "inner consistency of reality." There is no tale ever told that men would rather find was true, and none which so many skeptical men have accepted as true on its own merits. For the Art of it has the supremely convincing tone of Primary Art, that is, of Creation. To reject it leads either to sadness or to wrath. It is not difficult to imagine the peculiar excitement and joy, that one would feel, if any specially beautiful fairy-story were found to be "primarily" true, its narrative to be history, without thereby necessarily losing the mythical or allegorical significance that it had possessed. . . .
>
> Because this story is supreme; and it is true, Art has been verified. God is the Lord, of angels, and of men—and of elves. Legend and History have met and fused. But in God's kingdom the presence of the greatest does not depress the small. Redeemed Man is still man. Story, fantasy, still go on, and should go on. The Evangelium has not abrogated legends; it has hallowed them, especially the "happy ending." The Christian has still to work, with mind as well as body, to suffer, hope, and die; but he may now perceive that all his bents and faculties have a purpose, which can be redeemed.
>
> So great is the bounty with which he has been treated that he may now, perhaps, fairly dare to guess that in Fantasy he may actually assist in

the effoliation and multiple enrichment of creation. All tales may come true; and yet, at the last, redeemed, they may be as like and as unlike the forms that we give them as Man, finally redeemed, will be like and unlike the fallen that we know.[12]

Tolkien's words—especially his neologism for the death and resurrection of Christ, the "eucatastrophe," meaning, oxymoronically, a "tragedy with a happy ending"—capture the infectious enthusiasm he and Lewis had for this literary form and also prepare us to recognize and engage the spiritual insight we encounter on every page in Narnia. Later Lewis himself summarized his own convictions on the topic of how "myth" works in understanding the historical fact of the incarnation, not as the relatively recent convert as he was in 1931, but now as a completely persuaded and notable apologist for Christianity:

As myth transcends thought, Incarnation transcends myth. The heart of Christianity is a myth which is also a fact. The old myth of the Dying God, *without ceasing to be myth*, comes down from the heaven of legend and imagination to the earth of history. *It happens*—at a particular date, in a particular place, followed by definable historical consequences. We pass from a Balder or Osiris, dying nobody knows when or where, to a historical Person crucified (it is all in order) *under Pontius Pilate*. By becoming fact it does not cease to be myth: that is the miracle. . . . To be truly Christian we must both assent to the historical fact and also receive the myth (fact though it has become) with the same imaginative embrace which we accord to all myths. The one is hardly more necessary than the other. . . . Those who do not know that this great myth became Fact when the Virgin conceived are indeed to be pitied. But Christians also need to be reminded . . . that what became Fact was a Myth, that it carries with it into the world of Fact all the properties of a myth. God is more than a god, not less; Christ is more than Balder, not less. We must not be ashamed of the mythical radiance resting on our theology [emphasis, Lewis].[13]

Considering the role myth and fairy tale played in their mutual growth as thinkers and scholars, as well as believers, Lewis and Tolkien both regarded the fairy tale as perfectly suited as a vehicle for expressing eternal truth. It provided for Lewis in particular the perfect "canvas" on which to paint the "pictures in his head" that in words became the Narnian tales.

What Lewis observes of Tolkien's achievement in his original review of *The Hobbit* (published first in the October 2, 1937 edition of *The Times Literary Supplement*) could equally be said of The Chronicles of Narnia:

> The publishers claim that *The Hobbit,* though very unlike *Alice [in Wonderland],* resembles it in being the work of a professor at play. A more important truth is that both belong to a very small class of books which have nothing in common save that each admits to a world of its own—a world that seems to have been going on long before we stumbled into but which, once found by the right reader, becomes indispensable to him. To define the world of *The Hobbit* is, of course, impossible because it is new. You cannot anticipate it before you go there, as you cannot forget it once you have gone.[14]

The world of Narnia is inherently a spiritual world, a world informed by C. S. Lewis's Christian convictions and wise understanding of our fallen planet. He deftly uses the conventions of the fairy tale to depict for us a winsome and whimsical landscape that stirs our heart and directs our soul, mind, and strength toward heaven.

To inhabit that world, we must be poised to *receive*, not *use*, this grand story. In so doing, we come to see that first and foremost, Narnia, like Middle-Earth, is a world "you cannot anticipate . . . before you go there, . . . and cannot forget . . . once you have gone." Narnia is not an allegory requiring a one-for-one parallel with personages and events in the Gospels, but a "supposal," as Lewis reckoned it. What if the Son of God were incarnate in a world like Narnia—what would happen? How would the tale unfold, and how would we receive him this time? This is indeed the perfect rationale for retelling the Gospels as fairy tales, as Lewis articulates in his essay, "Sometimes Fairy Stories May Say Best What's to Be Said":

> I saw how stories of this kind could steal past a certain inhibition which had paralysed much of my own religion in childhood. Why did one find it so hard to feel as one was told one ought to feel about God or about the sufferings of Christ? I thought the chief reason was that one was told one ought to. An obligation to feel can freeze feelings. And reverence itself did harm. The whole subject was associated with lowered voices; almost as if it were something medical. But supposing that by casting all these things into an imaginary world, stripping them of their stained-glass and Sunday school associations, one could make them for the first time appear in their real potency? Could one not thus steal past those watchful dragons?[15]

Now that we have met Mr. Lewis, we are wise and brave enough, equipped to steal past those watchful dragons ourselves.

Off we go now. We've got bona fide passports and a visa to cross the border into Narnia; we're no longer mere readers of maps and guidebooks, mind you—we're visitors, explorers, really. It's our turn now to go through the wardrobe with Lucy and with Edmund, Peter, and Susan.

For there Aslan awaits.

Chapter 2

Finding What You're Not Looking For:

The Lion, the Witch and the Wardrobe, Chapters 1–3

We do not know what awaits us around any corner. The most familiar place may in fact be a portal to a new dimension; the most mundane object may be the instrument by which we enter a new world. Is there a faded map to stumble upon in an old, badly lit attic or cellar, pointing us to a secret destination heretofore unexplored? Might we be destined to become heroes or heroines in some mysterious otherworld yet still get home in time for supper?

That's the kind of breathless hope and stupendous wonder that the Pevensie children entertain upon being whisked out of wartime London to the safety of the countryside and a large old house over which a wise but not wizened, kindly old professor presides with a few of his house staff.

The circumstances which lead them there are not pleasant. Who wants to be driven from mommy and daddy, from our own beds and toys and storybooks and breakfasts, air-raids abounding, bombs falling overhead from a ruthless enemy? No, we would not choose to visit even the most inviting holiday spot under these conditions. We're worried about our parents! Why couldn't they come with us?

But we must make the best of it. We must show our parents that we can be mature and poised and brave. Or maybe just that we can get along for as long as it takes. And who knows? Maybe there will be adventure even yet; there are so many rooms and so few rules! The only possible downside, besides terribly missing mom and dad, is, well, we are stuck here with our brothers and sisters, and we all know what that will be like!

Peter will lord it over us because he's the oldest; and Susan will "Tsk! Tsk!" us to death because, like Mother, she knows it all; and Edmund, oh that Edmund, he will make sarcastic remarks all the time to ridicule and spoil our fun; and Lucy, poor old Lu, will be the brunt of Edmund's caustic monologues and come crying to us every minute of the day.

Just more of the same old same old, only worse, since we don't have school and our neighbors and the rugby field and the morning papers to distract us from the everyday-ness of their burgeoning character flaws. To be stuck in this house with all of them. And the only thing worse would be if it rains, too! What's that? It *is* raining? Rats! We will just have to look around inside our expansive playhouse!

We don't know what we are looking for, but we shall surely find it!

Lucy Looks into a Wardrobe (Chapter 1)

FIRST NIGHT

We're ten miles from the nearest railway station and two miles from the post office—landmarks of civilization and connectedness! But we have come here for refuge from London's trauma. This is not suburbia; this is the country. We're supposed to be isolated, out of harm's way, protected.

Imagine a large home with servants to cook and clean and make our beds! (Well, maybe we have to do that. This isn't a holiday, after all.) Our home in the city is so confining and cramped. We can almost "roam" this place and never find an end to it.

15

The sounds, the smells, the nooks and crannies: it is so much different from what we are used to. How did we end up here?

And the professor. How odd but friendly he is; his very features make us want to laugh. But he has a knowing look, part mischief, part cunning. His wink, his smile tell us something that he's not telling us. Almost as if he hopes we start exploring and discover something that he does not care to show us. Maybe it is something we can find only if we do the looking for ourselves?

Can a house be too big? Lucy thinks it's "creepy," but she's the youngest, with the most to fear, and no mommy-and-daddy room to run to when she's scared. Out in the countryside you can really hear nature, and you can hear things for the first time in your life that have not been muffled by buses and airplanes and trains. Lots of birds! And that owl Peter identifies is just the first in a menagerie of fowl and other animals we will encounter. Why does Edmund think, though, of *snakes*? He makes us nervous. A good night's sleep is what everyone needs. Edmund will still be here though!

WHAT THE MORNING BRINGS

Time to explore. Yes, there is a wireless and, my oh my, so many books! We thought our house had a lot of books, but the professor must be a real bibliophile. Could anyone ever read so many words? And if he could, how could he keep them all straight in his head? But we're not going to sit around all day looking at books, no matter how colorful or large or imposing they may be. A room-by-room inspection is in order. The books will be there when we get back. And who knows how long we will be with the professor anyhow?

Room by room. Pictures here, a suit of armor there. More books! And a big empty room with just a wardrobe—you know a big stand-alone clothes closet with two big doors and a mirror on the front. Most people put coats in them for storage—lots of mothballs. Nobody looks in a wardrobe because everyone knows what is in them. And, besides, the doors on wardrobes are notorious for being hard to open or shut. And if you ever get trapped inside one, good luck trying to get out. Especially if you are a little girl like Lucy. The youngest.

But when the others run out, looking for something more interesting than an old wardrobe, Lucy is the one who is curious and simply must find out if it is locked. It's not; what might be inside? (She thinks of everything and makes sure she leaves it open.) Oh that smell of fur, and how it feels when you touch it! Lucy loved it. (Of course, lots of folks nowadays would not be too happy that animals were being killed for their pelts, but back then such furs were common and certainly a luxury.) But what a deep wardrobe, since there seemed to be a second, maybe a third, row of coats. Surely she will bump into the back of the wardrobe. But wait. There is no "back" here. It just keeps going and going—to where? What is that crunching noise, spilled mothballs?

AT THE LAMPPOST

No, it's not coats and hangers now brushing her face but tree branches! What an odd thing to have in a wardrobe; really, the professor and his staff must be even odder than we thought they were. But it's getting colder and it almost seems like . . . it's snowing. Let's look over our shoulder and make sure there is a way back, and, yes—we can see the daylight peeking through the empty room we've just left. We can go back, but we won't. This is just too strange and appealing. It's twilight here, wherever "here" is. We would not want it any darker. But there is a light ahead to guide us forward.

Lucy is a brave little girl, wise well beyond her years, but maybe a tad reckless. But she has a pure heart and has a poise about her that breeds trust in others. She knows what she is doing, doesn't she? We want her to keep going, but we'll stay one or two steps behind, thank you very much. But still—this is a little risky. Taking it all in, the snow, the woods, the lamppost, what kind of wardrobe is this? But, of course, it's not a wardrobe anymore, or rather the wardrobe is just a portal to somewhere else. It's a different world—but whether inside the professor's house or whether the professor's house is "inside" it, who could tell?

But if we had any doubts about our topography (or furniture design!), all we have to do is look past the trees into the light of the lamppost. What kind of creature is that, small, demure, carrying an umbrella and some parcels? Goat legs. A man's chest and head. And a tail! What did they call these things in ancient mythology? Fauns! He's a faun. "Goodness gracious me!" (p. 8).[1] He talks. Great: a talking faun, just back from Christmas shopping. Stranger and stranger. Bombs in London. Talking fauns in the country. Which is stranger or more terrible?

What Lucy Found There (Chapter 2)

THE INTERROGATION

What do you say when you first meet a faun? It's not in the etiquette books, trust me. He is so courteous though, bowing as he does. He has great powers of observation, an educated faun to be sure. (What are faun schools like? And do they get recess?) Who should be more startled—Lucy or the faun? When two worlds meet, and these are the ambassadors for both, shouldn't they both be equally anxious about first contact? But the first thing out of his mouth besides "Good evening" is a pointed question: "Should I be right in thinking that you are a Daughter of Eve?" (p. 9).

It's understandable that Lucy does not understand him. He's not speaking like a faun should (however it is that they are supposed to speak!), but like an anthropologist or news reporter. It's an interrogation or interview, not a pleasant conversation between two new friends. If you've never been called a "Daughter of Eve" (or "Son of Adam"), you might not know how to answer either. And if you've never been accused of being a "girl" or a "Human," you might be a little off-kilter too. Abstract categories like "gender" or "species" are not usually used to make small talk in polite company. This faun is sizing Lucy up, not preparing a welcoming party. He knows what Lucy "is" in a detached, scientific, book-learning sort of way, but not as a person. He's heard of creatures like her, like you and me, but he's never seen one before. What accounts for his clinical curiosity anyway?

MEETING MR. TUMNUS

Casual greetings aside, it's time to move to real small talk and real introductions. Lucy we know. Who is "Mr. Tumnus"? A faun from—what is that, *Narnia*? Where's Narnia? Well, it's the land between "the lamp-post and the great castle of Cair Paravel on the eastern sea" (p. 10). Cair para-what? Anybody got a map? Time for a geography lesson. But it's not Lucy driving the conversation. It's Tumnus still. He wants to know how she got there, in Narnia, and all she can tell him is what we already know: she came in "through the wardrobe in the spare room," which he immediately mistakes for places on an atlas, countries he should have paid more attention to when he was in middle school. (How funny our conversations might be to those overhearing them, understanding the words or the sounds we are making but not the significance.) There is no "place" called "Spare Oom" or "War Drobe," but you can tell Mr. Tumnus is taking mental notes about all this (p. 11).

The line of questioning he pursues is not quite sinister but not quite generous either. But the invitation to tea is hard to turn down, even if it does seem to be getting late and we can no longer see the wardrobe door at the professor's house. It's summer back there but, it appears, winter here. So the prospects of a roaring fire and some toast and sardines and cake sound appealing. What could a few more minutes hurt? So off we go, trailing Lucy and her newfound . . . friend, to his, uhh, cave.

At least it's a clean, well-lighted cave. And by the light of the fire, Lucy can make out the titles of some of Mr. Tumnus's library holdings (what's going on: books, books, and more books—on either side of the wardrobe!), including one attention getter, *Is Man a Myth?* (p. 12). What if he is, or isn't? (The very thought of being the "subject" of someone's thesis or investigation is a little unnerving, as if one were on trial or had to justify or explain one's existence or value. Think of that the next time you are studying a "subject," and put yourself in the place of the person, place, or thing under scrutiny. It could make you edgy. "Knowing" is a personal, relational activity, not just the accumulation of facts and figures. We bear a relationship to what is being known, a responsibility if you will, not just to get it right but to respond to the knowledge we gain of people and things with integrity and respect.)

Where is this conversation going? Mr. Tumnus is in monologue mode, telling Lucy of what can best be called Narnia as it once was—idyllic life in the forest, midnight dances, cavorting with nymphs and dryads, hunting parties after the white stag who grants wishes to those who capture him, red dwarfs and their mines (p. 13). But that is all in the past; and Mr. Tumnus's guard is down, and he becomes self-forgetful, falsely cheerful, finally melancholy: "not that it isn't always winter now." It's during his flute recital that Lucy, who wants to laugh and dance and sleep and cry all at the same time, decides she'd better go.

Then here is a weeping faun out of control. This has all become too much for him to keep up the pretense of polite surface welcome. Lucy has not been there because Mr. Tumnus is such a great and generous host. He's a spy for the white witch. That's why he is so curious. That's why he is so inquisitive. That's why his first time in the company of a real daughter of Eve, conscience-stricken, he breaks down. We've only been in Narnia a little while, and already we know there's sweetness and light, and there's darkness and treachery afoot.

THE REAL LOWDOWN

Narnia's current state is easily summed up: "Always winter and never Christmas" (p. 16). That says it all. The price much of the world—certainly Europe and North America—pays to celebrate Christmas is enduring winter. When the snowflakes fall, sleigh bells ring—aren't you listening? At least Christmas is coming! The cold, the wet, the freeze, the ice, the gray-blue cloudy skies—we can make it through all that as long as we know Christmas will eventually arrive. It's enough to keep us going till spring, till the thaw that the new season brings. Christmas!

But in Narnia, Christmas has been banished. And that's not the worst of it, as Lucy finds out. Narnia is under siege by a wicked, self-appointed queen, a white witch who has divided the world of Narnia into two parts: those under her thumb and in her pay and those who hold out hope for the return of Christmas. There seem to be precious few of these out-holders!

Mr. Tumnus *is* a bad faun as he confesses, despite Lucy's protestations that he is not. She has been lured to his cave dwelling so that he can keep an eye on her and learn her story and whether there are any other humans about. He has pretended to be her friend so he can betray her to the white witch, lest he be mutilated, tail and horn cut off, hooves turned solid—or worse, turned to stone. That seems to be the main fate of those who would dare oppose her will.

But there is a glimmer of hope. Lucy has not been lulled to sleep, and she has a way back to the wardrobe. And a speck of light accidentally falls from the brokenhearted and downcast Mr. Tumnus, if you are paying attention. He tells us the white witch is on the lookout for humans, but there are four thrones at Cair Paravel to be filled that might somehow thwart her evil plans. What could that mean?

The whole wood is dangerous. Trees are listening too, and some are in the white witch's employ. Even if Lucy gets back OK, Mr. Tumnus is himself, so to speak, not yet out of the woods. She leaves behind her handkerchief as a comfort and as a token of her forgiveness of his intended treachery. Will she see him again? Panting, she reaches the wardrobe and hears the familiar voices of her siblings. "I'm here!" she shouts, assuring them that she is all right (p. 19).

Edmund and the Wardrobe (Chapter 3)

MISSING WHAT'S NOT MISSING

Have you ever been gone for a while from a place or a group of friends and thought you'd be missed, indispensable and social catalyst that you are? And then found out that nobody really noticed? Or they got along OK without you? How hard it is to try to convince someone who ought to have missed you that it is important to acknowledge that you're back! That's what Lucy faced when she trudged back through the wardrobe door into the empty room full of her siblings.

Narnia time is different from our world's time. That's the first important distinction between the two realms—oh, that and the fact that there are fauns who talk, treacherous trees, and a wicked witch who seems to control the weather. Hours spent in Narnia take minutes in England's time zone. And that makes it a little hard to maintain credibility with your two brothers and a sister who already regard you as a diminutive nuisance that can not slow down the rest of them if you turn out to be loony or sick or mentally challenged.

Her breathless recounting of her exploits—tea with a man-goat, snow in summer, a witch, what about "Narnia"—the name itself ought to stir images of a magic wardrobe! But no dice. They fling open the door, and it's just an ordinary wardrobe. An ordinary wardrobe! How cruel. That's what they all thought the first time they looked in the room; that's why they all ran out and Lucy stayed behind for a reconnaissance mission. But it's just an "ordinary" coat closet now, anybody can see that. Hide-and-seek is OK. A made-up story, that's OK. A hoax, that's OK. But claims of reality? A true adventure in another world? Sorry, that's not OK. Everyone knows old houses can be quirky and strange and creepy. But there are not "other worlds" lurking inside waiting to be discovered. The only explanation is "poor old Lu." She's off her rocker, as they used to say.

REAL HIDE-AND-SEEK

It's miserable to know you're telling the truth and can't prove it. There are two problems really for the truthful person, which Lucy clearly is. The first is, of course, one can make up stories if one wants to, but it is important that the distinction be maintained between someone who makes up magical wardrobes and alternate worlds for fun, for entertainment, and knows she is doing it—and those who actually make such journeys and discoveries! Lucy's imagination is as active and productive and creative as anybody's. But this is stuff, so to speak, you can't make up.

The second problem is that when you have told the truth, and understand the difference between reality and fancy, but others believe otherwise, they then begin to expect you to admit that you made the stories up, or else you will be branded a liar.

22

You see what you see; you could be wrong, have mistaken a dream for reality, or simply been misled. But you can testify only to what you saw with your own eyes and heard with your own ears. Being coerced into admitting something was merely imagined is worse than being thought crazy. Though that is quite unpleasant too. But to maintain her dignity, Lucy has no choice but to stand her ground, even if it invites continuing ridicule: Edmund "sneered and jeered at Lucy and kept on asking if she'd found any other new countries in other cupboards all over the house" (p. 23).

Push a person far enough, and she will go to any lengths to prove her innocence—even risking a return to a land she knows to be under the rule of a dreadful witch who turns rebels to stone. And that's what Lucy does the next wet day when playing inside is all there is to do. A new game of hide-and-seek erupts, and this enables her to get a second look into Narnia.

When she hears the steps of one of the others, she ducks inside the wardrobe, careful to leave it open a crack—since "it is very silly to shut oneself in a wardrobe, even if it is not a magic one" (p. 24). And who is it who would be her pursuer? None other than Mr. Nasty himself, Edmund, skeptic of skeptics and terror of little sisters. His motives are pure—that is, unalloyed, not noble: he wishes to enter the wardrobe to catch and prove Lucy wrong and to extend his reign of ridicule. He's "in" for more than he bargained for, to be sure. And because he is not as experienced in wardrobe travel, he foolishly closes the door solid.

By the time Edmund realizes that this is a most unusual wardrobe—the most unusual wardrobe ever made, in fact—it is too late. He is bound for Narnia, and prima facie evidence that Lucy is telling the truth after all. His wild groping can't find an exit other than the one Lucy discovered; his move toward the light brings him not back into the spare room but into the winter of Narnia, a world that looks to him for all the world as empty and silent.

The silence, the emptiness, in fact, is eerie to Edmund, and he calls ever more earnestly for Lucy, seeking her companionship—first apologizing to his absent sister, pleading for her to come and show him the way back, then abruptly grousing about her absence. Is the mighty, cool, calm, collected Edmund getting scared in a little game of hide-and-seek? Isn't it typical? The selfish and ego-driven find their identity in undermining others and then seek their victims out when they find themselves sinking further into dismay and turmoil. Then, when they are not rescued immediately, they blame others for their predicament. Edmund's final insult: "Just like a girl" (p. 26). The main trait Lucy has shown since her arrival is integrity, and it is characteristic of bullies like Edmund to demean those who have the qualities they most lack. Edmund, not Lucy, is the one found "sulking."

But there is someone waiting up ahead to answer Edmund's distress call. He first hears the bells far off in the woods. And then he sees the slight reindeer who pull the sledge that transports her majesty. He first sees her as "a great lady, taller than any woman" he had ever seen, covered in fur, her face extremely, utterly white, and not just pale (p. 27). He can't help see her as beautiful but also as "proud and cold and stern" (p. 27). In another place or another time, Edmund might have mistaken her for a queen who had come to offer him shelter from the terrible winter. In fact, he does mistake her for exactly that.

She is not sure, at first, even what kind of creature Edmund might be. (What is it about Narnia that the first question people ask is not *who* are you but *what* are you?) He responds with his name, his most precious possession, the name his parents gave him at birth and by which he had been called hundreds and thousands of times. He is no doubt wishing at this point someone dear to him was calling his name—even Lucy would do! But his name is not what this tall lady is seeking. She wants to know something else—does he not know how to address a queen?

Of course, Edmund does not know she is a queen. Edmund does not know a lot of things, and in his sputtering and backtracking, he can only blurt out that he's out of school and on holiday—as if his circumstances ("Hey, what is this, a quiz? I'm on vacation and I can't be expected to have answers to questions like these outside the schoolhouse!") gave him a special license for ignorance. The queen will not be assuaged: "What are you?" she demands (p. 28). We shall find out.

Reflecting on the Journey So Far

It is interesting to note the two contrasting entries into Narnia, Lucy's and Edmund's, and what they signify.

Lucy, under the same duress as the other Pevensie children, has maintained her poise, purpose, and integrity throughout their early exile from home. Lucy tells the truth, defends her honor, and expresses concern for others in an innocent and sisterly way. Edmund, by contrast, arrives at the professor's house in a surly mood, prone to exaggeration, ridicule, and coarseness.

How fitting it is that Lucy is the one who discovers Narnia first—and is the one who can empathetically and knowledgeably deal with the terrible plight of Mr. Tumnus, her would-be betrayer, and the devastation of Narnia and Narnians everywhere through the treachery of the white witch. Her immediate reaction is less concern for her own well-being than for Mr. Tumnus. And it is clear the effect she has on him. Having spent time with Lucy and having witnessed her sincerity and purity of heart, Mr. Tumnus has no choice but to renounce his mission and allow her return to the wardrobe. From putting her life in jeopardy, Mr. Tumnus has now moved to being willing to risk his own in order to ensure her safe passage. Such is the effect of noble, truthful, caring people on those who would otherwise cause them harm or distress.

Edmund, by contrast, is ill prepared for sudden adventure or dramatic changes of scenery. Simply put, he has neither the depth of character nor the maturity of outlook—let alone reason, imagination, and faith—to navigate Narnia successfully. Unless by "successfully" we mean ready to join hands with evil. Jealous by nature, and self-aggrandizing in action, his entry into Narnia spells trouble, and he quickly meets up with it. He is in Narnia only a few minutes before he encounters the very person from whom his sister has fled, the person responsible for the misery and sorrow expressed by Mr. Tumnus. It is telling that in Edmund's first encounter with the white witch he finds her face beautiful in its extremity: not just pale but "white like snow or paper or icing sugar" and highlighted by a "very red mouth" (p. 27). She is tall, yes, but towers above him and her dwarf driver and her reindeer, because they are so small. He has the perspective of a morally challenged young man, ill equipped to defend himself, let alone his fellow sons of Adam and daughters of Eve. Indeed, as we shall see, he feels very little solidarity with his brother and sisters on the other side of the wardrobe. If Edmund were an FM-radio station, he'd be "All Edmund All the Time."

And so we leave this scene at the end of chapter 3 wondering several things: Where is Lucy, and will she be able to bring help to Narnia and convince the others that her testimony is true. What has happened to Mr. Tumnus, since Edmund has come to the same lamppost where Lucy first met him and he seemed to be missing? And how will Edmund answer the white witch's question?

Some Background Notes

FLEEING LONDON

C. S. Lewis and his brother Warnie actually had children staying with them during World War II who were evacuated from London during the German air raids over the city. Oxford, where Lewis lived and taught, provided a safe haven since Germany's mad ruler, Adolf Hitler, had indicated a penchant for Blenheim Palace near Oxford, the birthplace of Sir Winston Churchill, as his residence should the Third Reich have won the war; he thus did not want his air force bombing prized property.

MR. TUMNUS

Mr. Tumnus is a faun and exemplifies Lewis's love of many traditions and myths, in this case, Greek and Roman mythology. Throughout the Narnian Chronicles, Lewis will employ character, image, and symbol from various mythologies in mix-and-match fashion. He is not, like his friend Tolkien, a purist about such things and does not mind a rich, even contradictory, tableaux of mythical creatures within the same story, no matter their origin or mesh with the story at hand. It's a "kitchen sink" approach that "Tollers" could not abide; he did not share the same enthusiasm for Narnia that his friend Jack Lewis had for Middle-Earth.

THE SONS OF ADAM AND THE DAUGHTERS OF EVE

Narnians refer to humans this way, and of course this is a reference to the book of Genesis, as well as the book of Romans and elsewhere—wherein we are told our origins as human beings. Adam, the first man, and Eve, the first woman, are united in marriage by God himself and together become the first parents. Their fall from grace is the beginning of our misery as a race and explains a great deal about why things have gone awry in our world. The apostle Paul takes pains to explain the consequences of Adam's sin and Eve's deception in his letters, particularly in Romans. The twist here, as we will find, is that Adam and Eve's children can play a positive role in helping redeem Narnia from its curse under the white witch.

NARNIA'S FALL

As we can discern even from the first three chapters, Narnia itself has experienced a kind of fall from grace but not to the extent that we have. The proof of this is that it is always winter and never Christmas. Evil has entered the world mysteriously through the white witch, only hinted at here in Mr. Tumnus's testimony. For now, let us just notice that in the mercy of Aslan, evil's spread has been mercifully restricted to the queen and her treacherous but perhaps coerced rebels. Rebels against whom? Aslan, of course, the benevolent king, and its true protector and king.

THE WARDROBE

This "ordinary" piece of furniture becomes extraordinary in the imagination of Lewis. It is Lewis's way of suggesting the transcendent and eternal are close by, "just around the corner," and that there are "portals" all about us that may be the "way in" to the sublime and the supernatural if we have "eyes to see." Its special history is learned by reading *The Magician's Nephew*. But it is better to learn about this after we have been through it once and not before.

27

The Lamppost

The lamppost is a landmark—a familiar sign of civilization but also a marker of where Narnia begins and ends. It is a visual map to the "Way back."

Narnia's Lost Boys (and Girls)

One who reads all the Narnian tales will note how often there are absent, ailing, or missing parents within its cast of characters. In *The Lion, the Witch and the Wardrobe,* the Pevensie children must live apart from their parents during the war; Digory, in *The Magician's Nephew,* is sent to live with his aunt and uncle Ketterley in their house because his mother is ill and his father is away in India; Prince Caspian's father is murdered by the treacherous Uncle Miraz in *Prince Caspian.* In *The Silver Chair* Eustace and Jill Pole are sent to Experiment House for their education by avant-garde parents whose connection with them is distant and arms' length, while King Caspian's sire, Prince Rilian, loses his mother to the evil of the green witch; and Shasta and his brother Prince Corin are separated at birth, and Shasta spends much of his life in exile, not knowing his true heritage or homeland in *The Horse and His Boy.*

Truth be told, this is actually a staple of much literature directed to children and was part and parcel of many of the stories Lewis grew up reading. E. Nesbit, already mentioned as a Lewis favorite, tries it out in *The Railway Children.* The total absence of parents or the children raised by a nanny or the runaway teenager or a mysterious mix-up at birth, and so on—these plot devices and circumstances inform many tales that allow young readers the free roam of imagination and the adoption of adult roles and personas by the children in the stories so liberated. Such stories answer the dangerous but perennial question: Hmm, what would I do if I could do anything, and my parents would not find out or care? James Barrie's *Peter Pan* and his clan of Lost Boys come to mind as one extreme answer to the challenge of transitioning from adolescence to adulthood. (Of course, it could be said, and some have, that such literature actually helps "invent" the very idea that there is a "transition" between adolescence and adulthood.)

Nevertheless, such a cast of characters and their woeful state speaks to something deep within Lewis's imagination and soul that motivated him to treat with special dignity and respect the separated or abandoned child and the alienated adolescent in these tales. We know from our discussion in chapter 1 how profoundly his mother's death and his father's withdrawal from his life affected him. Thus, in Narnia, often a surrogate mentor must emerge to play the role that a loving parent normally would: certainly Professor Kirke plays that role in *The Lion, the Witch and the Wardrobe;* Dr. Cornelius in *Prince Caspian;* Puddleglum in *The Silver Chair;* the hermit in *The Horse and His Boy;* Aslan himself in *The Magician's Nephew;* and a whole chorale of older, wiser sons of Adam and daughters of Eve in *The Last Battle.*

In the land of Narnia, "lost children" find their way home through Aslan's intervention. And in *The Lion, the Witch and the Wardrobe,* in order to be found, they must first realize they are lost—i.e., in trouble, in need of guidance, in need of hope, in search of joy. This is certainly Edmund's fate and crying need. This is indeed something the adult Lewis could reflect on—and narrate well—as he looked back on his own life.

Chapter 3

Turkish Delights and Other Tempting Confections:

The Lion, the Witch and the Wardrobe, Chapters 4–6

Here are we—in no faun's land! That is, without Lucy as our compass, without Mr. Tumnus as our host, facing a white witch who claims to be queen of Narnia, and our only ally, or at least our only known relative, Edmund, standing by us. At least, we think he is standing by us.

This is, to say the least, an interesting predicament about which the professor might exclaim, "What do schools teach these days?" But he is not nearby either. He's on the other side of the wardrobe. But who could blame any curriculum director of any school, for not including Wardrobe Ethics 101 or Narnian Politics 200 or Advanced Witchspeak? This is not what the schools prepare us for. But it may be what our parents instill in us to deal with at one stage or another in our lives these obstacles: uncertainty, ambiguity, conflict. Narnia now appears to be full of it. Some children are ready; some are not.

And age is not always a barometer of what can be successfully faced and overcome. The key character traits are honesty, courage, faith, hope, and love—all of which provide Perspective with a capital *P*.

In Narnia, the character we brought with us is the character we must employ. If we left the professor's house as spoiled, immature, and basically selfish, going through the wardrobe will not magically bestow selflessness, honor, or perseverance. The perspective needed to face challenges in or out of Narnia is that of the godly, confident, moral person who answers and asks questions with truth as the goal. Temptations for compromise and self-advancement at the expense of others will emerge; they must be resisted and conquered, sometimes on behalf of others with less perspective or backbone. This takes double courage: courage to act in integrity in the first place with everything on the line and courage to face the opposition of those we are trying to save despite themselves. Who am I talking about? Edmund, of course.

Turkish Delight (Chapter 4)

BEING EDMUND PEVENSIE

Having been accused of being a dwarf, Edmund musters enough self-respect to explain that he is a boy and has never had a beard. A boy! How feeble that sounds when it is spoken out loud. Edmund is a young man who probably boasted (or, at least, protested) again and again in arguments with his parents and siblings that he is a "man," at least a young man. And here he is, reduced to explaining that he is a just a "boy."

Boy is not a word used in Narnia, and the queen seizes upon its mention. "Do you mean you are a Son of Adam?" (p. 29). And "Son of Adam" is not a phrase Edmund has probably ever heard; he can't think of an answer. She might as well have asked him if he were the son of Zeus. But "boy" and "Son of Adam" are code words to her, and they mean one thing: "enemy"; for she has been on the lookout for, maybe centuries, the possible border crossing of sons of Adam and daughters of Eve who might unseat her. That is something she knows, something that makes her heart race—not something Edmund could possibly know or appreciate at this pregnant pause.

He cannot explain his whereabouts or how he got there except by saying he opened a door, which probably sounded as silly to the queen as it did to Edmund, he who just a few minutes before was mocking his sister Lucy for her crazy imagination. People don't just walk through doors into other worlds, do they? At least before this moment, Edmund never thought so. But he is suddenly aware that proving Lucy wrong is the least of his challenges; he has every reason to fear what may be pending for his continued health and safety. He has had no practice in reading the actions or interpreting the motives of witches. It is hard to know whether to pity him or tell him, "I told you so."

The sudden shift in the queen's tone and verbiage is alarming—one moment she is calling him an idiot and looks like she may just kill him, the next she is comforting him, out here in the cold with no coat and, worst of all. Nothing warm to drink! Poor Edmund, her good little . . . boy. And so, out here, in the middle of nowhere (all Edmund has seen is a lamppost, a forest, snow, and the queen's sledge—for him Narnia is nothing more than a staging area for terror so far), the queen will host a little dinner party. What is she doing with that bottle of hers? That drop of liquid produces a jeweled cup that bears a beverage that warms him to his toes—and time to ask the fateful question, *Would he like something to eat?* (p. 31).

What's this? Edmund doesn't skip a beat? It's like he's been waiting for weeks for someone to ask him just this question so he can say, "Turkish delight, please." Turkish delight, please! What nerve he has; he recognizes neither the gravity of his peril nor the consequences of his actions. His sister is missing, and he is clearly in the presence of someone very, very strange and menacing. Yet somehow he regains his poise and can calmly request Turkish delight. Astounding! And then, *voila!* the queen loosens another drop from her magic bottle, and a neat little package appears of several pounds of the best morsels he has ever tasted.

If Edmund's powers of discernment had ever been exercised, if they existed at all however atrophied, he might have noticed that in some ways the Turkish delight tasted *too good*. It refreshed him too much. So much, in fact, that he fails to notice how he is being positioned to answer the queen's questions, almost like he is being drugged to reveal secrets he might in his right mind resist. The sad thing is, it is not clear that Edmund would resist divulging secrets even if he weren't being bought off by Turkish delight. To resist he would need to have at least one iota of concern for someone besides himself. It does not appear that that iota is available to him.

The interrogation that might have to occur under hot, bright lights or under torture in some laboratory setting occurs effortlessly under the spell of Turkish delight inside the very sledge that he feared entering moments earlier. Out the information comes precisely, specifically, unguardedly: yes, he has a brother and two sisters, there are four humans, count 'em—four. Two sons of Adam, two daughters of Eve. Four. She must verify this. Four, no more and no less. This "means something." And Edmund could care less as long as the Turkish delight keeps coming; he even forgets to call the queen "Your Majesty," but she doesn't care either. She has what she needs for now. She is set for the pitch.

"Son of Adam, I should so much like to see your brother and your two sisters. Will you bring them to me?" (p. 33). *Son of Adam* is now an honored title by which she addresses the callow Edmund. He'll try, he says, if there is more Turkish delight in the offing. Only at her house, but even bigger prizes await someone as valuable and resourceful as Edmund. Can you believe this? Edmund is princely material. If he will only bring the wayward siblings to her castle, he can someday be king. No, this is not to be believed, but sadly Edmund is in no condition to think straight. And he looks to all "neither clever or handsome" (p. 34). He would become king *now,* getting his hands on that Turkish delight pronto. But he is missing the point; even the queen underestimates his ego when she tries to sweeten the offer by adding his brother and sisters as duke and duchesses. He protests: "There's nothing special about *them*" (p. 35).

For her plot to work, all Edmund has to do is be himself. No special treachery is required on his part. Though he possesses some dim sense of the queen's subterfuge, the prospect of reigning over his own realm, and getting all the Turkish delight he can imagine, is enough incentive to say whatever he needs to say to get this bounty. He doesn't even hesitate to pledge to keep it all a big secret between him and his newfound monarch. He will go on his way back through the wardrobe as the queen's one-person public relations staff, denouncing the evil gossip that fauns might spread and enticing his siblings to her lair.

MEETING LUCY

The last person Edmund wants to see now is Lucy. Coming from the opposite direction, Lucy cries out, "So you've got in!" (p. 37). She thinks it's grand; he thinks it's terrible. There's explaining to be done—and it's all his. His halfhearted apology is waved away by Lucy, who must rush to tell him of her new encounter with Mr. Tumnus, relieved that the wicked queen had not exacted revenge upon him. Edmund is startled; how could he possibly cover up his new covenant with the white witch. He pretends ignorance (something he does not have to practice much): "The White Witch, who's she?" (p. 37).

Lucy has the complete picture. The white witch is wicked; she's not to be trusted even though she calls herself the queen—all of Narnia that is true and right and noble rightfully hates her for the havoc she has wreaked in their land. She has the power to keep it always winter, never Christmas; she turns creatures to stone—the facts keep mounting. Surely anyone can see that such a person is not safe to be around. Something must be done! And Edmund, of course, does not want to hear it. Who are your sources, he challenges; ah, the last refuge of a scoundrel: malign your research! When she reveals it's none other than her friend, Mr. Tumnus, he reverts to simple racism, an attribute that must be common to him even back in London: "You can't always believe what fauns say" (p. 38). "Everyone knows it. Ask anybody you like."

So onward we go, back through the wardrobe, back into the empty room, Lucy thinking the best, Edmund thinking the worst and feeling the worst given the pound of Turkish delight not settling well in his stomach. Lucy feels vindicated and is excited about the prospect of sharing the news with Peter and Susan. Edmund is already plotting his cover-up and his continued deception under the employ of the white witch. How I wish we could tell them all what we've seen and heard!

Back on This Side of the Door (Chapter 5)

LOYAL LUCY BACK ON TRIAL

You know, it's not that easy, just telling the truth and waiting to be believed. That's what Lucy again finds, right in front of us, and how dreadful that her own brother, Edmund, can't be trusted. It's not a reversion on his part, just an extension of the boy he already is. Lucy, however, is unprepared for the ferocity and conscienceless declaration that she is, once again, making it all up. "Oh yes," he tells his audience, "Lucy and I have been playing—pretending that all her story about a country in the wardrobe is true" (p. 41).

You and I would be beside ourselves (or I would be beside me, and you beside you, I mean) with this betrayal. And, look, so is Lucy. She cannot even speak and rushes from the room. Before her older brother and sister she is once again callously attacked and called a liar. Surprisingly, at last! Peter accuses Edmund of unusual cruelty and meanness. At least somebody is taking up for Lucy, even if he is concerned about her reveries in the wardrobe. Peter sees through Edmund what we have already seen in person, "You've always liked being beastly to anyone smaller than yourself; we've seen that at school before now" (p. 42).

Lucy won't back down; we knew she wouldn't. But this only increases our anxiety about what might happen to her next. Maybe it doesn't matter if they just all stay out of Spare Oom and the War Drobe? But that won't do. We know, and she knows, and, above all, Edmund knows, there is a land inside or through that wardrobe and some terrible or glorious fate awaits the inhabitants of Narnia and one Pevensie child in particular. It's just a matter of when. The only thing to be done is to take it to the professor. He'll know what to do.

WHAT DO THEY TEACH THEM AT THESE SCHOOLS?

We still don't know a whole lot about him, do we now? He is a friend of the Pevensie parents, and they clearly trust him enough to send their prized progeny off to him for safekeeping, and maybe just a little tutoring on the side. But he remains a mystery. We don't even know why he may be called a professor. A professor of what, anyway? Is this a self-designation, or does he actually teach somewhere? Or is he now retired to sit at home in this cavernous house to read or maybe to write books? We shall not find out much before we have to trust him. And we actually first hear him speak as this crisis arises. Our greatest hope, of course, is that he can somehow help Lucy restore her good name.

But he does more than that. He first pays them the tremendous compliment of listening to what they have to say, patiently and quietly without ever interrupting them. We have to pause to reflect on that and how remarkable it is. Most adults have a hard time listening to children or adolescents period, let alone without interrupting them. The professor knows and understands children, even though he apparently has not ever had any of his own. He recognizes they need to know that they are important, that their words should not be dismissed, and that it is only by paying attention to them that their respect can be earned and maintained.

And his first words could hardly have surprised them more: "How do you know that your sister's story is not true?" (p. 43). Exasperation ensues. Of course Lucy was just pretending—even Edmund said so. And as soon as Susan says this, she realizes how unreliable this bit of testimony probably is, even before the professor points it out: Which is the more credible, trustworthy, honest? The answer is *Lucy*, without question. But the professor is just getting started because he has much further up and further in to go in demonstrating the kind of discernment necessary to fare well in Narnia. Almost as if he might have been there himself once.

When the talk turns away from Lucy's veracity to her sanity, the professor is on the offensive. He dismisses talk of her instability with a flourish: she does not exhibit the features associated with madness. And now Susan is getting worried since she's never had a grown-up talk like this before, but the coup de grâce is just ahead. "Logic!" the professor cries out, "Why don't they teach logic at these schools!" (p. 45). There are only three options, based on what they know, so he surmises: (1) Lucy is lying; (2) Lucy is crazy;

or (3) Lucy is telling the truth. The most logical conclusion, absent further evidence, he tells them straightforwardly, is that she is *telling the truth*.

Neither Susan nor Peter has ever heard an adult say such things—namely, that it may be more logical to believe in another dimension, another world inside a wardrobe, mind you, than to disbelieve it! How amazing! They are so used to having their testimony gainsaid automatically, it is astonishing to hear these words. Peter is having none of it since he himself had investigated this alleged portal: "But how could it be true, sir? . . . If things are real, they're there all the time" (p. 45). The professor's simple and curt reply, "Are they?" told them more than they could ever have imagined about his own knowledge about the house, the wardrobe, and Narnia—even though he claimed to know "very little about it."

His disposition on how much time might or might not elapse on one plane of existence while inhabiting another sounded, well, too well informed not to be offered as a serious defense of Lucy's main alibi. Peter's final plea, "But do you really mean, Sir, that there could be other worlds—all over the place, just around the corner, like that?" gets a decisive affirmation from the professor, "Nothing is more probable" (p. 46).

Nothing is more probable. A shocking but consistent answer from the only one who could have been expected to shed light on their collective predicament. Lucy is gotten off the hook, and Edmund is called on the carpet, and minding one's own business is the order of the day.

BACK TO THE WARDROBE

Without saying so, the four Pevensies had quietly let the topic of the wardrobe drop; Edmund has every reason to try to get back but not at the cost of his own reputation being further impugned. Lucy, no doubt, is worried about Mr. Tumnus's fate but isn't about to subject herself to another round of conjectures about her truthfulness or well-being. And, well, Peter and Susan are somewhat under scrutiny themselves as the older siblings who are expected to keep order and behave well. Having had the professor pull the rug out from under them by refusing to end the speculation about Narnia, they are none too keen on starting up their own rumors.

No, people are just going to settle into one corner or another and while away the time until they can return home. A good plan, until a new group of tourists shows up to walk through this rather famous house of the professor's that is written up in all the guidebooks. Having had enough of Mrs. Macready's barbs about not interrupting her and of staying out of the way of her touring troupe, the four dash all over until finally settling on waiting them out in the supposedly spare room and duck into the wardrobe to escape the nosy and impertinent invaders to their adopted home. Oh, Peter, last one in, did you remember not to shut the wardrobe door?

Into the Forest (Chapter 6)

LUCY REDUX

It's full circle now. First it was Lucy, then Lucy again followed by Edmund, and now all four of them find themselves through the wardrobe and into Narnia proper. It is no longer a game of hide-and-seek or someone pretending to find a whole new world or questions about Lucy's sanity. It's cold. And branches are poking their backs. This is not your grandmother's wardrobe. It's daylight and no one is asleep. This is real. This is true. And Peter and Susan are doing all the talking. Edmund is strangely silent. Lucy was right all along. And there's nothing to do but apologize. "Will you shake hands," Peter says (p. 51). Of course, Lucy forgives. And they set about exploring the wood in the fur coats they have been rummaging through every time they hide out or pass through the wardrobe.

Who's to lead? Well, Lucy of course—she has been there twice already and knows her way around. It's just slightly embarrassing that Edmund forgets to pretend that he *hasn't* been there and slips by offering some directional counsel when it appears they would not be headed to the lamppost, the only landmark Edmund knows well. When this faux pas points to Edmund's overbearing lies, Peter rebukes him, and Edmund privately vows to provide payback for his troubles.

Oh, Edmund. Has he forgotten about his pact with the queen, his craving for Turkish delight, the promise of a throne? Not a chance. Not for a minute. All he needed was the right time and the freedom to line things up his way. The professor was only a temporary obstacle. How fortunate for Edmund that the tourists had shown up. He did not think it would be this easy to get them all in the wardrobe at once.

FINDING MR. TUMNUS

It was only logical for the four children to locate Mr. Tumnus for an update. Lucy leads the way since she knows where he lives, but from a distance it looks bad. What's that ahead? Oh, no, a terrible surprise. The door has been ripped off Mr. Tumnus's cave; it's cold, dark, and, worst of all, empty of Mr. Tumnus! Things smashed about, it's clear someone has been here who had no particular affection for Mr. Tumnus! But there was a note, with an official-looking letterhead; what does it tell us? Let's go out into the light to see what it says.

Uh-huh, it's the queen all right. She's arrested Tumnus for crimes of high treason, which, translated, just means he didn't report Lucy's arrival to her secret police when he should have. And look at the honorific titles this white witch signs off with: *"Imperial Majesty Jadis, Queen of Narnia, Chatelaine of Cair Paravel, Empress of the Lone Islands, etc."* (p. 55). The "etcetera" is hers; she lays claim to any and all current and future titles. Is that an ego or what? Not that there is anyone around to impress. When all are in your employ, under your command or else, who is there to win over or melt down? Who is there left to admire you on your own merits so to speak? If you are commanded to love her and obey her, what could love or obedience even mean?

These are the questions Lucy is asking, and maybe even Peter or Susan. But Edmund? He's just got to find a way to hide his real allegiance until it is too late. And Susan is not much help because after Lucy explains what is going on, her impulse is just to get out of there and go home. Home. Home? What home? Back at the professor's weird and magical house? Who knows what else awaits them there? No, Lucy pleads with them and with us: we can't turn our backs on our friends. Mr. Tumnus risked his life for Lucy's, and now they must do something to help or rescue him. That is what friends do for friends (p. 56).

Lucy's moral gravity is contagious, at least for Peter and Susan. They must mount a plan of action. Edmund is not so sure. Or, rather, he is very sure that he wants no part of them. But they can't just do nothing. Where to turn? The intuitive Lucy knows—what's that over there, a robin, a trustworthy bird. Everything else is so strange and unnatural, but birds can talk, or at least understand daughters of Eve. Lucy pleads, show us the way to Tumnus the faun. It really does look like he wants us to follow him. Shouldn't we go?

And so we do. For at least a half hour. But Edmund needs a private conference with Peter. What in the world could he have to say about all this? You can't trust robins. What was that? You can't trust robins? How in the world would Edmund know something like that? Peter properly corrects him: robins are always good birds in all the stories. Robins couldn't be on the wrong side. Books won't mislead us, and the tales we grew up hearing have the ring of truth about them. Trust robins, I tell you. They'll be on the right side.

This isn't going well. The last card to play is to question, "What is the right side, anyway?" That Edmund, he's a smooth operator. "How do we know that fauns are in the right and the Queen . . . is in the wrong?" he opines (p. 59). Don't listen, Peter. You can't trust this guy. But we don't need to tell you that, do we? You've said it yourself. Edmund has a reason for everything he does; there are always strings attached. The faun saved Lucy, you say? Did he? Did he really? Who can verify that?

And so it goes. Lost. No supper. What else could go wrong? On the other hand, from another point of view, the robin's, what else could go right?

Reflecting on the Journey So Far

Surely every child loves stories, even scary ones, but if so, preferably told by a loved one, slowly, with emphasis on heroes and heroines, their bravery in the face of implacable villains, courage in the midst of opposition, hope in the face of despair, rescue in the midst of danger. The longer and the more twists and turns the better. The truth is, one does not have to "grow up" and leave behind this childhood longing for real truth and triumphant heroes glimpsed through the veil of story. These traits may emerge even in adulthood. And even adults can dread the lights out, the darkness, the occult, the boasts and spells of witches.

Witches are meant to scare us—to evoke in us fear and trembling—for they represent the dark side of life. Biblically witches are not divided into white and black categories; there are no "good" witches in the Word. Thus, Lewis is comfortable leaving the mysterious white witch as she is in these pages without a lot of commentary. Witches are neither invincible nor indefatigable. Lewis does not have to tell us she is evil. Of course she is; she's a witch.

This may seem harsh in a time of political correctness when there are organizations and conventions and lobbying groups who champion the causes of "good" witches. The truth is, it is not harsh—just straightforward. The reason there are "witches" who dabble in the dark arts, who cast spells, who seek to gain power over the elements and over the souls of those whose eternal destiny hangs in the balance is that they have turned their backs on the order of heaven. They resist, as did their mentor Satan, the power of God to create, and as G. K. Chesterton, a great influence on C. S. Lewis, once said: when men cease to believe in God, they do not believe in "nothing," they, in fact, believe in "anything." That is, they will latch on to any explanatory worldview, dogma, or practice that frees them from having to behave in any certain way, believe in certain things, or make decisions based on some higher rule or authority. Their task, their daily bread as it were, is to undermine all authority, whether natural or supernatural, temporal or heavenly, and to wield power over it for as long as they can in order to gain as much independence and freedom as possible in the short time that they will have "lives." And a short time it is.

And yet somehow the vampire figure, now well into the twenty-first century, is offered by some as a paradoxical symbol of vitality and "eternal life." It is nothing of the sort; it is a sad mockery, a pathetic reverse image of what both true life and eternal life really are. Vampirism and witchcraft do not prolong "life"; they, in fact, prolong dying. They exemplify every nonliving, noncreative, unhealthy lifestyle.

The white witch herself is just such a forbidding creature, whose power exists only to manipulate others. When she meets Edmund, she recognizes however dimly the echo of the threatening prophecy that sons of Adam and daughters of Eve will sit on the thrones in Narnia—something ringing in her ears from centuries ago. Edmund may be a human, but she is really not sure until he tells her. Her senses, dulled by her own drunken power, her own disequilibrium reigning over her emotions, having practiced evil and thought only of herself lo these many years—these alone keep her from immediately killing the child. She instead offers him the false hospitality of coming to her lair.

Queen Jadis, however, has a fatal flaw, as all villains do. It's called pride. Edmund has this flaw too, and only supernatural intervention will keep it from being fatal for him.

Some Background Notes

TURKISH DELIGHT

There is such a thing as Turkish delight, a confection, a candy that is popular around the world, but especially in Turkey and in the Middle East, where it was born. It has no magical powers and does not cause any sort of addiction—or at least no more than any sugary candy or gelatin! Also called "lokum," Turkish delight has been made out of various ingredients, but usually water, sugar, corn starch, cream of tartar, and rosewater, combined often with nuts and fruits, then baked, cut into small rectangles, and usually sprinkled with powdered sugar. Here, of course, it comes to symbolize a temptation, a particular draw for Edmund that would cause him to betray even his own flesh and blood to get more of it. The more he has, the more he wants—and while he is eating it, it is delightful. Like all temptations, when succumbed to, the initial thrill or elation soon fades and one is left sickly and empty of stomach, heart, and soul.

THE PROFESSOR

We do not learn much about the identity or the past of the professor in *The Lion, the Witch and the Wardrobe.* One must turn to *The Magician's Nephew* for this information, and it is well worth waiting for. *The Magician's Nephew* was written toward the end of Lewis's series, and so the true story behind the wardrobe and the professor's own knowledge of and experience in Narnia were not settled until near the end of his composing process.

What we can say is that he is inspired in part by Lewis's tutor, William Kirkpatrick, "the Great Knock," who taught him about logic and debate and clear thinking. One can hear an echo of something he must have said to Lewis while under his charge in chapter 5: "Why don't they teach logic at this school?" To learn more about the Great Knock, consult Lewis's autobiography, *Surprised by Joy*, especially chapter 9, appropriately entitled, "The Great Knock." Lewis ends that chapter with these words: "My debt to him is very great, my reverence to this day undiminished" (p. 148).

LIAR, LUNATIC, LORD

One of the more distinctive features of Lewis's essays and teaching mode is his use of what is sometimes called "the trichotomy," a three-part version of the philosophical term known as a "dichotomy." It is basically a technique to dramatize for an audience that there are only three real choices or options in assessing the truth value of a proposition. It attempts to force a choice: a dilemma is a forced choice between two options; a trilemma is a forced choice among three. Lewis comes by this way of argument from his favorite theologian, St. Augustine, who employs it in his fifth-century work, *The City of God*.

The professor uses it here to compel Peter and Susan to think "logically," to see that even in their own estimation, the possibilities for explaining Lucy's aberrant (to them) behavior boil down to three: she is (1) lying, (2) mad, or (3) telling the truth. Put this starkly, the professor hopes to convince them that the only "logical" conclusion is that she is telling the truth about her adventures in Narnia.

Interestingly, this is parallel to the way he defends the divinity of Christ in his apologetics work, *Mere Christianity* (New York: Touchstone Books, 1996). Sometimes referred to as the "liar, lunatic, or Lord" argument, Lewis uses it analogously to the professor's defense of Lucy in this passage, which is his climax to a chapter-long explanation of the Gospel accounts of Christ's claims to be the Son of God:

> I am trying here to prevent anyone saying the really foolish thing that people often say about Him: "I'm ready to accept Jesus as a great moral

teacher, but I don't accept His claim to be God." That is the one thing we must not say. A man who was merely a man and said the sort of things Jesus said would not be a great moral teacher. He would either be a lunatic—on a level with the man who says he is a poached egg—or else he would be the Devil of Hell. You must make your choice. Either this man was, and is, the Son of God: or else a madman or something worse. You can shut Him up for a fool, you can spit at Him and kill Him as a demon; or you can fall at His feet and call Him Lord and God. But let us not come with any patronizing nonsense about His being a great human teacher. He has not left that open to us. He did not intend to (p. 56).

Chapter 4

Hospitality Is as Hospitality Does:
The Lion, the Witch and the Wardrobe, Chapters 7–9

Well, a fine fix we're in. Our guide, the robin, has fled, and none of us really knows the way back, not even Lucy. Talk about strangers in a strange land. Who knows who or what lurks around the bend? The white witch's spies are everywhere, and you can't even trust a tree in these parts. A tree! Peter and Susan are completely new to Narnia, so they are no help. And Edmund? He'd as soon turn us in to Fenris Ulf, the queen's henchman, as help us find a way home. He's got Turkish delight on the brain. Worst of all—we're hungry! How will we get dinner!

Let's not panic. We must maintain our poise and, most of all, our hope. We want to make mom and dad proud of us. Narnia may seem cruel and cold and terrible, but something tells us that there is still something good about this place. It's just buried deep. If even Mr. Tumnus can gain the courage to save Lucy, all is not lost! And why would the professor, who's trying to help our parents keep us safe and who went out of his way to defend Lucy, let us loose in this house and let us find the wardrobe if it were utterly dangerous and full of misery? It's almost as if he wanted us to find Narnia. He knows something he can't tell us, something we have to discover on our own. Maybe we're supposed to find the wardrobe, and maybe we are supposed to get lost in the woods?

That's a crazy thought. Why would it ever be good to get lost? Maybe so we can be found? Stranger and stranger still. Adults are always warning children about not going too far, not stepping off the beaten path. But not the professor. He doesn't seem to put a lot of stock in being safe and careful. That's exciting and scary at the same time. An adult who thinks like a child! Maybe when he said we should "mind our own business," he really meant, "You ought to get to the bottom of this yourselves!" That professor. He knows something he's not telling us, but he must have a very good reason.

A Day with the Beavers (Chapter 7)

ON THE TRAIL

Wait a minute. What's that? Susan's spotted something, something moving. Something trying not to be seen. There, over there. Oh, no! Another animal. We've seen a half man, half goat, we've seen two miniature reindeer, and we've seen a dwarf. Now what's this?

A beaver. A beaver calling us to come over to where he is! Signaling us to be quiet and careful. What do we have to lose? As Susan says, "It's no good standing here and I feel I want some dinner" (p. 62).

"Further in, come further in. Right in here. We're not safe in the open" (p. 63).

Oh, my. This beaver can talk!

"Are you the Sons of Adam and the Daughters of Eve?" (p. 63).

Here we go again with the interrogation! Our reputation precedes us. It seems that everyone, good or bad in Narnia, has been expecting us for who knows how long. But we've got to keep our voices down. The trees, you know.

The beaver won't even speak her name. *You know who*—the queen. "There *are* trees who would betray us to *her;* you know who I mean." Leave it to Edmund to be rude. How do we know what side you are on, he asks, thinking to himself, "What side am I on! This is getting dicey!" And then the beaver shocks us all, pulling out that handkerchief—the one Lucy gave Mr. Tumnus as a "token" (p. 63). His explanation seems plausible—Mr. Tumnus asked him to meet the children here (wherever "here" is), show them the hanky, and take them to— And then he starts to whisper so quietly with those mysterious nods of his punctuating each syllable that we have to creep closer and closer to hear: "They say Aslan is on the move—perhaps has already landed" (p. 64).

Whoa. That name. Aslan. A-S-L-A-N. That name uttered so quietly and reverently in his raspy voice, so boldly, so confidently. That name—ASLAN! It makes our hearts beat faster. It makes us think of wonderful things, great things, glorious things. Like the best dream we ever had. Like the most haunting melody you've ever heard. ASLAN. Hearing this name creates some kind of special energy or blessings or courage. Every one of us, Peter, Susan, Lucy—wait, every one of us, except one, Edmund—feels new hope. Edmund instead feels "a sensation of mysterious horror" (p. 64). ASLAN.

And then suddenly the name has drifted into the air as all sounds do, and in the silence we are shaken out of our reverie, and we are squarely back to our dilemma. What do we do? Mr. Tumnus is gone, imprisoned somewhere, and we must talk about a way to help him. But not here, not now. This is too risky a place to have a strategy session. And, besides, we need our supper! Off we go to, well, the beaver's house. House? The faun's house was a cave. What could this be like? Whatever—it's an hour through the thickest parts of the forest at a quick pace. Who knew beavers could travel so fast? But he knows these woods. (And he does not have to bend over like a human to duck those limbs and branches!) He seems to be someone we can trust with our whole hearts. He knows ASLAN. He said, "Aslan." What could that mean? Who is Aslan?

Ah, good, a clearing ahead, valley below it, and a river below it—frozen. It's always winter now! And what's that—of course, a dam. Beavers make dams! And this one is superb, and the beaver is so proud! "Merely a trifle. . . . And it isn't really finished!" he says modestly (p. 66). Cute! But where's supper? Oh, over there in that, uhh, charming beehive with the smoke coming out. So that's where beavers live. At last, someone is cooking! Hope it's for us!

That's what we're all looking at and hoping for . . . except Edmund, who looks up and around and notices something completely different. The two small hills. The ones that demarcate his own palace, where his throne awaits, and, more importantly, his Turkish delight.

SUPPER AT LAST!

Well, the beehive looked closer than it was. And the way we have to walk the dam as a pathway to the entrance to his house was not styled for humans, of course, icy and slippery as it was; but if you're hungry, you'll find a way to navigate it! Mind that "nasty drop" on each side, and whatever you do, don't look down. At last we're here. Beaver hospitality!

How grand to be announced as if we were royalty: "Here we are, Mrs. Beaver. . . . Here are the Sons and Daughters of Adam and Eve." It's *Mr.* and *Mrs.* Beaver, is it! So, not only do beavers in Narnia talk; they get married, too! A she-beaver, sitting at her sewing machine, supper on the stove. (Now where would a Narnian house-beaver get a sewing machine? From a catalog? Hmmmm.) But what did she mean, "To think that ever I should live to see this day!" (p. 68). This day? What's "this day"? Was she expecting us? But how could she? We didn't even know we were coming. Just a couple of hours ago, when the robin left us, we were lost. Stranger and stranger still!

How easy it is to fish when you're a beaver! Well, it's not fishing exactly, but it's only fitting that Peter, namesake of that great fisherman of the Gospels, should go with Mr. Beaver to capture the rest of our meal. Never seen a more beautiful trout! How different the inside of their most hospitable home was from Mr. Tumnus's. No books (that *is* unusual!), just utilitarian stuff—stuff you use to cook, to build, to fish, to make a living, and to make a life. These beavers are industrious and creative and earnest in their simplicity. And in their faith. Hospitality is just who they are. Winter after winter after winter—they get by, hoping against hope, and then, one day, "This day," comes: the day the sons and daughters of Adam and Eve arrive. Their faith has been rewarded.

What a feast! Potatoes! Fresh fish! Marmalade rolls! Creamy milk! Beer (for Mr. Beaver, *only*)! Finally, tea! We sigh, with great contentment. We're warm. We're fed. We're safe. Now to business.

What Happened after Dinner (Chapter 8)

BACK TO TUMNUS

Lucy's been waiting all evening to ask. And now it bursts forth: "Do please tell us what's happened to Mr. Tumnus" (p. 72). Indeed. It is hard to know how much time has passed since Lucy and Edmund were last in Narnia. Anything could have happened. Mr. Beaver knows only what a little bird told him, literally, of course. northwards. Anybody got a map? He says it like its significance is self-evident. Oh, yeah, northwards. That means, that means . . . well, what does that mean? Susan demands to know. "I'm afraid it means they were taking him to her house," Mr. Beaver intones (p. 72).

"Her house." Even though no one has spoken of it, everyone in the room, especially Edmund, knows what this means. Mr. Tumnus has been taken to the white witch's house, the place few creatures return from. Rumor has it that her courtyard is filled with stone statues—statues that were once living, breathing Narnians. Sounds pretty hopeless. But mustn't we do something! Atta girl, Lucy!

Nope, Mrs. Beaver, explains, there's nothing to be done, not because she doesn't want to be cheerful—but you just don't walk up to the witch's door and knock, and say, "Dear Ms. Witch, would you please let my friend Mr. Tumnus out to play?" Peter won't go down so easily, either; there must be some trick we can play, dress up and pretend, and she'll let us in, and . . . Ah yes, pretending. Just what they thought Lucy was doing when she pleaded with them to believe that she had been through the wardrobe. But pretending won't do now, no matter how good they may be at it. No mere ruse will work. This is a witch we're talking about, the kind who can keep making it winter and never Christmas. The kind who can turn people to stone. The kind who can make hot drinks and Turkish delight out of a few drops dripped from a magic bottle. No, rescuing Mr. Tumnus will take something more than pretense or wishful thinking. Things are desperate, yes. "But now that Aslan is on the move—" (p. 73).

Not Safe, but Good

There's that name again. *Aslan*. ASLAN! Here comes that feeling again. Feelings of good news. Of spring! How can a name alone bring such excitement and expectation and hope. ASLAN!

Let's get right to it. Who is this Aslan? Susan wants to know. We all want to know. Ah, you can tell Mr. Beaver has been saving this moment since we got back to his warm abode—saving it so he can savor it. *Who is Aslan?* This is the world's greatest—ahem, this is Narnia's greatest question. The sons of Adam and daughters of Eve have come to the right place at the right time to get the answer to that momentous question.

Mr. Beaver tells us like he's waited his whole life to say just this: "Aslan? Why don't you know? He's the King. He's the Lord of the whole wood, but not often here, you understand. Never in my time or my father's time. But the word has reached us that he has come back. He is in Narnia at this moment. He'll settle the White Queen all right. It is he, not you, that will save Mr. Tumnus" (p. 74).

Oh, my. If we ever needed to hear something to cheer us, to elevate our spirits, this is it. ASLAN! A king! A lord! Just as we are letting this resonate in our hearts, Edmund casts gloom: Maybe the witch will just turn him to stone, too! Thanks a lot, Edmund. You really know how to spoil a mood. But Mr. Beaver just scoffs the way someone who has just heard something completely ridiculous scoffs! "Lord love you, Son of Adam, what a simple thing to say!" (p. 74).

A simple thing to say! This Aslan—and we hardly know more than his name, and the few titles Mr. Beaver gives him, lord, king—is more than equal to the task. And we believe him. Why just listen to that infectious rhyme Mr. Beaver recites by heart:

> Wrong will be right, when Aslan comes in sight,
>
> At the sound of his roar, sorrows will be no more,
>
> When he bares his teeth, winter meets its death
>
> And when he shakes his mane, we shall have spring again (pp. 74–75).

Wow! Go Aslan! Right the wrong! End our sorrows! Bring spring! ASLAN! And then suddenly, you pause, and you start thinking about the other words in the rhyme. Roar? Teeth? Mane? Hmmm. What kind of king are we talking about here? I mean, I know it's Narnia and all, but it almost sounds like we are describing . . . wait a minute.

OK, let's add this up. Captured faun. Wicked queen. Treacherous trees. Hospitable beavers. And what kind of king? Oh, boy. Just when we thought we were getting a handle on the players in our scorecard, we're set for a jolt. "You'll understand when you see him," Mr. Beaver assures (p. 75). See him? OK. That's the whole reason Mr. Beaver brought us here—to meet him. Him? So he must be a man, right? Lucy says.

Mr. Beaver, so jovial and exuberant to this point, is now stern. "Aslan a man!" he's almost shouting. "Certainly not. . . . Don't you know who is the King of the Beasts? Aslan is a lion—*the* Lion, the great Lion" (p. 75). Well, in Narnia, you just never know who you're going to meet. But we can be reassured, can't we, that, lion or not, he must be "safe"? I mean, who wants to "meet" a lion? We know what a lion does. No one would be stupid enough just to walk up beside one and chat about this or that. We could be breakfast, lunch, and dinner!

Mrs. Beaver doesn't help matters, does she? You've got to be *brave* or *silly* to "appear before Aslan without their knees knocking" (p. 75). Hmmm. Those are the two choices? Brave or silly? Where's the professor? He's good at "trichotomies." Isn't there a third choice? Then Lucy once more pleads, "Then he isn't safe?" (p. 75).

Come on now. We're looking for encouragement here. We've traveled a long way today through wet, snowy, sloppy, dark, and brooding woods to join the company of a couple of beavers who have fed us dinner to strategize how to help our friend Mr. Tumnus. And now they're telling us that we can't do a thing to help him, but Aslan can. And Aslan is not a man. He's a lion. *The* lion. So it's only fair for us to ask again: he's safe, right? We're humans, dash it all, not Narnians! But Mr. Beaver is emphatic: "Safe? . . . Who said anything about safe? 'Course he isn't safe. But he's good. He's the King. I tell you" (pp. 75–76).

Oh my. He *is* a lion. *A real lion.* Aslan. Think about it. Of course, he's not safe. Who could expect a lion to be safe? Domesticated. Docile. Tame. Then he wouldn't be a lion at all. But we don't want a safe lion, do we? This is not a zoo. I mean, if he's going to save Mr. Tumnus, save Narnia, he's got to be fierce and strong and terrible. He has to have a roar that brings fear and trembling to everyone—the wicked and the faithful. He has to be a lion in all the *lion-ness* he can muster.

But there's something else puzzling in what Mr. Beaver said. He's not safe—OK, that we understand. He's not safe, but he is "good." Good? How can a lion be "good"? Good in what sense? Good for whom? Good for what? Good by what criteria? Good at being a lion? Well, we expect at least that much from our lion kings, thank you. But Mr. Beaver means something more than that. Maybe more than he can tell. *Aslan is good, but he's not safe*. We don't know what this can possibly mean, but it is somehow comforting. Goodness is something in short supply in Narnia right now, and it seems like it's all headquartered right here in this little beehive of a beaver home. Goodness is good enough for now. We will trust that Aslan is good. Even if we don't know what that means. Even if we are scared to meet him.

THE BETRAYER GOETH

And meet we shall. That has been the whole point. That's what Mr. Beaver is saying. Down the river we'll meet at the stone table. Hmmm. That sounds a little ominous, doesn't it? *Stone* is just not a happy word right now. So we meet Aslan at the stone table. How will that help? We're getting impatient, especially Lucy. And just then, Mr. Beaver unleashes one more rhyme, and this time it's about us, we sons and daughters of Adam and Eve:

> When Adam's flesh and Adam's bone
> Sits at Cair Paravel in throne,
> The evil time will be over and done (p. 76).

Oh, *that* Cair Paravel! The one Mr. Tumnus spoke about. But wait a minute, what is Mr. Beaver saying? We're here, and somehow, our being here means it's the beginning of the end, since none of our race, Adam's race, humans, has been in Narnia before. That we are supposed to go to Cair Paravel and sit on thrones. But that can't be right.

What about the queen? She's got to be human too. I mean she is already on a throne, with three to spare.

What's that? She's claims to be, but she's not . . . human? Then what is she? And Mr. Beaver's explanation deepens the whole mystery of this place, tying our world and his together. The queen is *not* a daughter of Eve. She's come from the line of Lilith. *Lilith?* Adam's first wife. Whoa. This didn't make it into the history books either! The queen is borne of the "Jinn" and of "giants." No human blood in her! (p. 77). This is getting stranger and stranger. I don't even want to ask more about this. Some things, some dark things, seem better left alone. What we do know is bad enough. A wicked queen, a witch, has seized a throne to which she has no rightful claim, and now, in order to keep it, she's turned all of Narnia into a big ice prison.

She's smart—or at least wary and selfish and vindictive, three traits that help keep scoundrels the scoundrels they are even better than being smart—and knows something about prophecy and whom to look out for. Humans! Four of them. Oh, yes. That's the whole point of her interview with Edmund, right! Now it's getting clearer. When the sons of Adam and daughters of Eve—the four of them—sit on the thrones at Cair Paravel—the queen's reign will end. And not just her reign, her very life! No wonder she is so determined! Wow. Edmund, did you hear that? Do you realize now why we needed to pay attention to the faun, and the robin, and why Mr. and Mrs. Beaver. . . ? Wait a minute. Edmund? *Where's Edmund?* We'd better find him. He might be in danger!

Mr. Beaver is calm and collected. No rushing around for him. He knows perfectly well what's going on. We don't need search parties, he tells us, because he knows exactly where Edmund is. *With the witch.* How does he know? He knows the truth in the same way the professor knew that Lucy was telling the truth about the wardrobe. He knows a betrayer in Narnia when he sees one because he sees something in the eyes, some mark of the witch, and what magic food he's eaten at her hand. How discerning this "simple" but wise beaver is, and how easily he confirms his unwelcome suspicions by a few simple questions: Has Edmund been in Narnia before, alone? And did he say whom he's met? (pp. 80–81). Yes. No.

Voila! No doubts. He's with the witch, and the only thing to be done is to stay away from her. She will keep Edmund alive to lure the rest of his clan to her palace. The last thing Peter, Susan, and Lucy should do is try to rescue him. So all is lost? Never. *Aslan is on the move.* And too must we be, for Edmund has gotten the witch on to us, and we may have only twenty minutes or so before she arrives with her secret police. On to meet Aslan, the lion king, who's not safe, but he's good.

In the Witch's House (Chapter 9)

WALKING A MILE OR TWO IN EDMUND'S SHOES (WITHOUT A COAT)

Put yourself in Edmund's shoes. Well, not because he deserves any sympathy from us, of course. But, really, we do need to look through his eyes a bit. When you're on the trail of a betrayer, even if he's your brother, it's good to do a little homework, of anticipating his moves and those of the dark side. He's a chap who's in deep, way too deep. He's lied and lied again. He's deceived and deceived again. Even he has trouble keeping his story straight. But now he's got to play it all out; what choice does he have? He's betrayed his brother and sisters; he's had a bellyful of beaver hospitality, heard all about Aslan and how bad the queen is; and now he has slunk away on foot up to the twin peaks of his captor's palace, driven all the way by his insatiable lust for more Turkish delight. There's no going back. That's the way evil feels. No way out. Might as well stay the course. He sees no path back to hope or valor.

Oh that Aslan. The name itself—and those horrible rhymes!—sickened him as much as the taut feeling in his stomach, craving, craving, craving "bad magic food" (p. 84). But how bad could the queen be? Surely not as bad as the witches in the storybooks? The queen wouldn't really turn his family to stone, would she? I mean, what are the genetic consequences of being half jinn and half giantess? (Even if Edmund had paid attention to his biblical history, and he didn't, there's no way for him to know the answer to this question. Genesis only tells us how *we* sons and daughters of Adam and Eve got here. And there's no proof that Edmund even knows that much!) To himself Edmund's thoughts are clear and rational and logical. But they are really egotistical and

54

nasty and mad. That's what happens when one gets trapped in the web of one's own lies and deceitfulness and cowardice. One ceases to be able to distinguish evil thoughts from righteous ones. And it gets worse.

It's one thing to rationalize one's own behavior; what's more dangerous is rationalizing the hateful, murderous, treacherous behavior of others in order to help justify one's own. No matter how Edmund twists it, the fact is, he's in league with a malignant and malevolent sorceress, whose motives and motivations devolve into one simple plan: hold on to power at all costs! Imagine Edmund thinking even for one minute that the queen is the rightful ruler of Narnia. Or that she could be better than "that awful Aslan" (p. 86). No, it doesn't last more than a minute, "for deep down inside him he really knew that the White Witch was bad and cruel" (p. 86).

But it was a long journey without a coat up to her small castle, and all that could keep him fueled forward was the ridiculous prospect that indeed he might become a king, that and his hatred of Peter, whom he thought of every time loads of snow fell on his back. And what would be the first act of his royal highness? Of all things: "decent roads" (p. 87). How practical and dutiful. And then of course, acquiring his own movie house, a few cars, and setting up the railways. Why, by the time he'd gotten to her house, he'd thought up lots of capital improvements to Narnia. Just like a county engineer or investment banker or mayor. Nothing too good for Narnia under his rule. All very rational and logical. Except of course that he was standing in the middle of a terrible winter night caused by a wicked and maniacal queen who has ruined a perfectly beautiful, peaceable world by her treachery and hatred. Making the railways run on time is just the sort of thing that dictators find so ennobling. He forgot the most basic question: where would a Narnian take a train to, anyhow?

This is the "problem of personal evil" in a nutshell, exemplified in Edmund's heart of darkness, an ego that knows no end and congratulates itself on its little concessions to "civilization" while running a worldwide jail for its inhabitants. Little treacheries, first thought, then planned, finally executed, day after day, throughout his childhood have now transmogrified into a giant hole in his soul. He whose nastiest was once just a sibling irritant now can effect evil that will devastate a whole world. There was (wasn't there?), once upon a time, a clean conscience and a healthy vision for Edmund. But that was long ago. So long ago that sulking has replaced thinking. He would not recognize goodness if he saw it (and, of course, he had many times over in Lucy, the professor, the Beavers). He can no longer discern right from wrong, falsehood from truth, white from black. He's the perfect capture for a white witch to use as a tool of destruction.

A Different Kind of Hospitality

How did I ever get here? This was the malingering question that occupied him in the stillness just inside the gate that was protected by a fierce lion just steps away from the door he feared to enter. As he stood motionless for who knows how long before the stone lion he mistook for a living one, he realized he'd forgotten that it was his accomplice the queen who was responsible for this dreadful scene. A stone graveyard. She turns all manner of beings into stone, and she's at work on him too. Unrepentant, he's cheered by the thought, horrible to any sane person, that maybe this rigid cat is Aslan the lion king: "She's caught him already and turned him into stone. So that's the end of all their fine ideas about him! Pooh! Who's afraid of Aslan?" (p. 91).

Who's afraid of Aslan? Edmund should be. And the queen surely is. For, you see, Aslan is *not safe.* Even worse, especially for stone-hearted folks like Edmund and the queen, Aslan is *good.* Their reunion scene is hardly joyful, is it?

"I've come, your Majesty," said Edmund rushing eagerly forward.

"How dare you come alone?" said the Witch in a terrible voice. "Did I not tell you to bring the others with you?" (p. 94).

Edmund can hardly get the rest of his "good news" out—that he's done the best (really, the "worst") he could and has them "holed up" in the Beavers' "safe house." (Slowly it has dawned on him that his hoped-for Turkish delight "prize" is not forthcoming. Neither is the warm drink. Nor any sort of warm welcome.)

But he still has more news, not so good: Aslan has landed. It falls on her ears with a tangible thud. The queen is not amused ("If I find you have lied to me . . .") and has no time to waste on further "pleasantries." Imagine that—the queen's ethics demand that there be no "lying"! Oh but she must act immediately. "Make ready our sledge," she orders, using the "harness without the bells" (p. 94). She plans a sneak attack.

Oh my. She's on to them, and Edmund is also clued in to just how single-minded the queen is in ending all threats to her throne. Maybe, just a little, in the back of his head, Edmund is beginning to thaw himself. Maybe, just slightly, a healthy dose of reality is meandering back into his consciousness, if not his conscience. Or, if not his conscience, whatever gland hosts his personal survival instincts. He knows he's in trouble. And he's got nowhere to turn. The people who might care about him and would try to help, well, he's turned them in. He's trapped. The queen's house, unlike that of the Beavers, is not a house of warmth and care and truth. It's a house of serpentine plotting and hopeless desperation. Edmund's a boy, just a boy, a human. And that fact's never been more precious nor more perilous to him.

Reflecting on the Journey So Far

Two famous phrases are uttered about Aslan in *The Lion, the Witch and the Wardrobe,* and both come from Mr. Beaver. One comes in this chapter ("Course he isn't safe. But he's good. He's the King, I tell you.") and one in chapter 17 (He's "not like a tame lion"). Both come in the midst of explaining something about who this mysterious lion is, whom we will learn eventually from *The Magician's Nephew* is the creator of Narnia. In *The Lion, the Witch and the Wardrobe*, we learn that he is its savior too.

Aslan is Lewis's most compelling authorial creation, someone who exemplifies all of the majesty, glory, courage, and grace of Jesus in a direct and consistent way. And, of course, this is no accident since Lewis intended to write a story on the premise that we might understand and cherish better the life of Christ if we could see it unfold in a different sort of incarnation, not as a man, but as a lion. (Why, someone could write a whole book about Aslan just analyzing this theme.[1])

In this emerging portrait, Lewis not only offers a stirring rendering of the character of Christ, as viewed from a third person (or "third beaver") point of view, but also the effects of even Aslan's name on those who hear it. As the narrator explains the children's response to the mention of his name, he reminds us that it is like "some delicious smell or some delightful strain of music had just floated by" (p. 65). This is parallel to an equally entrancing statement Lewis makes about the call of heaven in his most beloved and most famous sermon, "The Weight of Glory": "The scent of a flower we have not found, the echo of a tune we have not heard, news from a country we have never yet visited."[2] It is the language of longing—of the deeply resonant song of grace and hope that emanates from the love of the Father, the incarnation of the Son, and the intercession of the Holy Spirit. Hardly any twentieth-century (or for that matter, twenty-first-century) writer captures so well the experience of being sought and loved by our Father in heaven. Yet, Lewis would tell us, it is a central concern of the ancient and medieval Christian tradition and one which he is simply continuing.[3]

It is not only the goodness of Aslan but also the psychology of evil that is explored here. Lewis has not only done us a great service in rendering innocence and goodness in his fiction; he also is adept at showing us the heart of evil, as he does in painting the contrasting portraits here of Lucy and Edmund, and Queen Jadis and Aslan. He has had some practice in depicting the motivations and machinations of wicked and devilish characters in his earlier science fiction tales, *Out of the Silent Planet*, *Perelandra*, and *That Hideous Strength*, but particularly in his famous 1942 work, *The Screwtape Letters*. This collection of intercepted "infernal correspondence" between a senior tempter (Screwtape) and junior tempter (Wormwood) reverses our worldview perspective (from above to below) in a clever way, analyzing the strategies and tactics of hell in trying to claim the soul of a young man.

In the end, they lose because their "Enemy" (Christ) is stronger and wiser than they and, most important of all, selfless. In creating Screwtape, Lewis has laid bare before us the brazen selfishness of Satan ("Our Father Below"), his servants' profound "inhumanity to humans," and, ultimately, his calamitous ignorance, for Screwtape never really understands Christ's tender care for the sons and daughters of Adam and Eve. He cannot therefore outwit Christ because he would have to outlove him, which is impossible. Lewis said *Screwtape* was both the easiest and the hardest thing he ever had to write—easy because he could just look into his own heart to see its lurking evil, and hard because in getting so close to the psychology of evil, he could "smell the brimstone."

Lewis offers a telling treatment of the character of Satan in his book about Milton's *Paradise Lost*, entitled *A Preface to "Paradise Lost"* (Oxford: Oxford University Press, 1942). His description of Milton's Satan (but equally applicable to the biblical devil), written in the same period as *The Screwtape Letters*, is an apt epitaph for Queen Jadis and all who would willingly follow her: "To admire Satan, then, is to give one's vote not only for a world of misery, but also for a world of lies and propaganda, of wishful thinking, of incessant autobiography" (pp. 102–103).

This is, indeed, a chilling thought, and one that we must guard against not only in Narnia but in our world as well.

Some Background Notes

ASLAN

"Aslan" is the Turkish word for "lion." Lewis, as a master philologist, both a lover and a historian of words, was familiar with many ancient and classical languages. "Aslan" gives the Narnian lion king an exotic-sounding name, mysterious and otherworldly. We can understand why it had such a profound effect on the children—for good or ill—when Mr. Beaver first utters it. It is not just a "magical" name; it's a holy one.

THE BEAVERS

Mr. and Mrs. Beaver are the first set of "talking beasts" we meet. They represent one of the many links to Lewis's childhood fascination with the possibility of conversing with animals and what insight they would share on our world. They are humble and noble, simple but wise—and very courageous.

Chapter 5

Aslan on the Move:
The Lion, the Witch and the Wardrobe, Chapters 10–13

It is time for some good news, isn't it? This is the longest uninterrupted stretch of time we have spent in Narnia, and it's been strenuous and exhausting and dispiriting through and through. Remember that old song, "Over the river and through the woods"? Well, we've followed a robin and a beaver through woods, valleys, rivers, a dam, more woods, valleys, rivers—you name it. The lamppost is a distant memory, and the wardrobe, well, let's just say that we never want to hear the words *hide* and *seek* in the same sentence again. Still, not all is lost. There is some light, some hope. We're meeting Aslan. Aslan!

The beavers' confidence is enough to sustain us for a little while longer, and that may be all we have. Is this a dream or a nightmare? We thought bombs falling on London was nightmarish, but now we've lost a new friend and our own brother to a witch, and we have no idea how the story will end. But Mr. Beaver keeps telling us that Aslan will come through and that he will need our help. Us helping a lion, can you believe it? But I guess, as the professor might say, "Nothing is more probable."

The thing is, we have no other choice. We have to trust the Beavers, and we must put all of our hope on Aslan—Aslan, that wonderful, awesome name. Aslan is on the move. And all about is the evidence of that; the snow is melting. The temperature seems to be rising. Can Christmas be far behind?

The Spell Begins to Break (Chapter 10)

JINGLING BELLS

Here we go again—moving about as fast as we can; and, thank goodness, Mrs. Beaver thinks well on her feet, or paws, or whatever it is beavers have. She's packing us supplies for the journey, which must be started very quickly indeed. We'll be on foot, and the queen will be on her sledge. There's no hope apparently that we will get there first, but we may get there smarter. And as soon as Mr. and Mrs. Beaver stop arguing about how much to carry with us and which path to take, we'll be on our way. I mean, really, we can't take that sewing machine with us!

And what's this now? The snow has stopped falling, and the moonlit pathway through the valley will keep us out of the sight lines, and certainly the reach of the queen since you can't take a sledge down there. Faster, faster! Move, move, move! Oh, no, it's snowing again (good for covering our tracks and our scent!), but we are so tired. And Mr. Beaver's tail is all we can see a foot in front of us. Where is he going?

A beaver hideout! What will these beavers think of next? A place of refuge and repose for a few hours. We do need rest. Desperately. How funny that Mrs. Beaver laments that we didn't think to bring some pillows. I guess beavers rarely travel so light! Ah, now to some much-needed sleep.

Only to be awakened by a startling sound. Bells. Jingling bells. Oh, no. It's the witch. Her sledge is here; she has found us out, and we are undone. Mr. Beaver, that courageous, intrepid Mr. Beaver goes out to have a look and—where is he? Oh, no! Conversation! Who is talking? Hmmmm. It doesn't sound menacing. What's going on? How strange. But not nearly as strange as what we would see when we came out of the hideout. Who could have expected this "nasty knock for the Witch!" as Mr. Beaver put it? (p. 102).

It *was* a sledge after all. And reindeer, real reindeer! But not, you know, hers—but, his. *His?* Why, Santa Claus, of course, or, as he is far better known in England, Father Christmas! Talk about some good news! Everyone knows what this means. Winter is fading, and Christmas has come! Father Christmas has come, "at last!" he says, since "Aslan is on the move," and "the Witch's magic is weakening" (p. 103). All of us were thinking the same thing—how often in our childhood memories Santa was fat and jolly and funny—but here, in Narnia, he was all that, but more than that, jolly, yes, but serious too, and especially *real*. And that reality evinced a seriousness about his task of gift-giving and of celebrating not his own coming but someone else's. And it made the children both "glad" and "solemn" (p. 103).

That's the thing about our world, isn't it? Things that are truly real often seem to be less so than the manufactured reality served up by the media and even the virtual reality our own imaginations sometimes cook up. What's really real, what's really solid and enduring and eternal, can be obscured or obliterated by the bleat of the image machines that churn out artificial reality, and we begin to trust in and even prefer the artificial to the genuine. Just think about the wonderful food and drink we have had in Narnia from Mr. Tumnus to the Beavers, and how poor old Edmund has been captivated by magic food, which is not really food at all but some kind of spell to make us think we've had nourishment when all we have really filled our stomachs with is empty words.

A BOUNTY OF GIFTS

But here standing before us is the real Father Christmas, and he makes us feel solemn inside not because we are not joyful or do not understand the significance of what his coming means but because there is something serious and sobering about the truth when it descends upon us. It's a strange and profound feeling to be witnesses of the reality of something we only have dreamed of or thought was a mere myth. It's strange and profound to discover that something this good and this glorious could really exist beyond our wildest dreams. Reality is always better than the false and the artificial, even if it is painful. Because reality, even in a world that possesses magic, is stronger than the made-up and the wishfully thought. And we could not have imagined anything like this—the real Santa and that he has really brought gifts! For everyone! (Everyone here anyway.) If he's the real Santa, of course there would be gifts!

Let's see. There's a sewing machine for Mrs. Beaver (he'll drop it off on the way past their place—locked or not, he's not going to be deterred); a finished dam and a sluice gate fitted (to help regulate the water flow—important for beavers and all Narnians) for Mr. Beaver; and presents for each son of Adam or daughter of Eve, "tools not toys" (p. 104). Peter gets the sword and shield perfectly shaped and sized for him. Susan gets the bow and quiver of arrows—to be used in "great need"—and a horn to blow whose sound brings help no matter what. And, finally, a diamond bottle of healing cordial and a dagger for self-defense for Lucy (p. 105). Wow—equipped for battle and equipped for healing in the aftermath of battle. This real Father Christmas knows how to give good gifts to his children! But wait, there's more: "a large tray with five cups and saucers, a bowl of lump sugar, a jug of cream, and a great big teapot all sizzling and piping hot!" (p. 105). Nothing could have tasted better or come at the more perfect time. And away he went as swiftly as he came, undaunted by the threat of the witch or anything else. For, as he said, "A Merry Christmas! Long live the true King!" Ah, the true king, Yes! Tea! Ham! Bread! Famished no more, we'd better be off to meeting the true king then!

Aslan Is Nearer (Chapter 11)

STALE BREAD

Timing is everything. While Peter, Susan, and Lucy were enjoying the company of Father Christmas and his gifts for them and the Beavers, Edmund was absent and in the presence of the queen. "In the presence of the Queen!" It sounds like it should be so noble and chivalrous, yet it is so terrifying. Royalty should breed respect and awe, not fear and horror. And so his special welcome-back "meal" was not the Turkish delight he'd so eagerly anticipated but "dry bread." Now her captive not her colleague, Edmund would be off in the sledge to the stone table where he'd stupidly told her the son of Adam and daughters of Eve would be meeting Aslan. But she had time for one more royal command to Fenris Ulf: "Go at once to the house of the Beavers . . . and kill whatever you find there" (p. 109). That's not an assignment you can interpret positively no matter how rosy your glasses are.

No, Edmund can no longer pretend that somehow this is going to turn OK for him or his family. No throne. No Turkish delight. All he has left are these thoughts boiled down to two words—*what if?* Over and over as the sledge ride goes on hour after hour: what if? What if he'd been less selfish, less greedy, less hateful. What if he'd told the professor what he's seen and asked his advice? What if he trusted and honored Peter, Susan, and Lucy? So mournful is he that he'd even be happy to see Peter. Oh, even Peter! Maybe the whole thing was a nightmare he could wake from, even indigestion that could be ended by the morning light. But just as Peter, Susan, and Lucy had a stirringly real encounter with Father Christmas, now Edmund has faced his own reality head-on. The queen is a murderer, and he has helped her track down his family. Willingly! Oh, the name of Aslan starts to take shape in his head. *Oh, Aslan, whatever you are, wherever you are,* Edmund is thinking, *I hope you're real!*

On and on and on they race. And, suddenly, there is a stop. Not a stop for breakfast (my, there is a lot of attention paid to food in Narnia!) but to the spontaneous Christmas parties that had emerged with the Father Christmas tour of Narnia—the news spreading furiously. A party in the queen's domain? Celebrating what? With whose catering? Their gaiety, good humor, and high spirits were ominous to the witch. Under her rule, Narnians are not so joyous or spontaneous. Only the free and self-governing can be "spontaneous." Something was terribly, terribly wrong. She demanded to know what the meaning of this was. At first nobody had the courage to speak, but then the witch uttered her usual threats, and finally the fox stammered that it's all come from Father Christmas! Oh my—other than Aslan—there was no worse name that could reach her ears. Liars, she says, hoping indeed that they are lying to her. Yet she knows they're not and gets a confirmation by a young squirrel who is too gleeful to deny it, "He has—he has—he has!" he cries out to all who can hear (p. 112).

This was all she needed to be provoked; and with a wave of her wand, despite Edmund's impetuous pleading, they were instantly stone statues. No leniency for spies and traitors, she declares; Edmund could not help but notice that, indeed, that was what he was, not to the queen, but to his own family, and to Narnia. And he felt something he had not felt in so long he perhaps had to pinch himself to make sure it was really him thinking the thought: he "felt sorry for someone besides himself" (p. 113). The thaw indeed had begun in Edmund's own heart. But too late?

Spring Erupts

The sledge races on but seems to get slower and slower and not because the reindeer are getting tired. It's the changing weather pattern. The snow is wetter, and then it is not falling at all. It is not as cold as it was. And it's foggy—a sure sign that there is a warming trend. The streams were bubbling. All there is is slush. This is a thaw! A Thaw! The place where it is always winter and never Christmas is having Christmas today, and winter is waning! The queen is not amused, again. Her driver, the dwarf, can offer no comfort to her, and he dispenses with any pretenses. To her consternation, he tells her that in the sledge they will never overtake the beavers and the children, so they must walk. So the forced march begins, Edmund's hands tied, his feet slipping, a whip at his back to keep him moving briskly and more briskly.

All of nature seems to be rejoicing, more green and blue everywhere you look from ground to sky. Narnia was awakening from its sleep. The colors were astonishing. The birds filled the forest with song. This was not a good omen for anyone campaigning for the queen. If anyone at all could be said to be "for the Queen," I mean. For the rest of Narnia, hope was abounding, and even the dwarf had to resign himself to the inevitable: "This is no thaw. . . . This is Spring" (p. 118). Even worse, "This is Aslan's doing."

That exclamation point was not lost on or welcome to the Queen. "'If either of you mention that name again,' said the Witch, 'he shall instantly be killed.'" Ah, the name of

Aslan, powerful, mighty, purposeful. Even Edmund now must place his hope in it. And if he can't say it aloud, he can say it in his heart.

Peter's First Battle (Chapter 12)

THE LION COMES

Miles away we have embraced that same blooming, buzzing order of springtime in Narnia as much as the unfortunate creatures whom the witch has turned to stone. We love it to the same degree that the queen and her crew have dreaded it, "The whole wood passing in a few hours or so from January to May" (p. 120). Who knew this realm could be so beautiful and clear and clean and fruitful. It felt like Eden to them, morning yet on creation day. That was how it was when Aslan came to Narnia. And how could we have anticipated this beauty? We are learning hour by hour more and more about just how treacherous the queen's hold on Narnia has been. But it's a good lesson to us that while evil can dwell and dominate for many, many years, the first bright burst of freedom and truth can bring forth redemption; joy and hope and love flow out in no time at all. And so it was being played out literally before them as the land and its creatures are restored to their former grandeur and peace. The river's currents now thawed and freely flowing demand of us more agility and careful navigation, climbing and panting and climbing again.

But it's to the stone table we head, and the name of this place still sounds ominous and forbidding. If only we can see Aslan, and sooner rather than later. And then suddenly right before us is a green open space where we can spot a forest in every direction but one, and finally to the East we see something moving. Oh, to have father's binoculars now! It's the sea and in the "very middle of this open hilltop was the Stone Table" (p. 121). And what a sight when you looked at it closely with its strange alphabet and a pavilion pitched on one side with its banners, one of which bore the image of a red lion. It's Aslan's throne! With these sights and the music, it was becoming overwhelming; and then, without warning, we got to see what we'd come to see. *The lion.* Aslan is here!

He stood in the center with other grand creatures from Narnia, not just fauns and beavers, mind you, but dryads and naiads and centaurs and a unicorn and, and . . . such wondrous sights! Too wonderful to behold and yet too majestic to take our eyes off them. Until, of course, we fix our eyes on him, on the lion king in whom we have put all our hopes. Until we have come face-to-face with the one whose very name has kept us alive these last few hours. It's his eyes and that golden mane . . . who would not go "all trembly." Who could dare to speak, to move toward him? Who has the courage to be the first? We look around waiting sheepishly—surely Mr. Beaver will do the introductions.

Mr. Beaver, remarkably poised, nudges Peter. But he hesitates—shouldn't the noble Narnians who have waited so long for rescue be first? No, it must be the son of Adam. Why not ladies first? (Never has Peter been so self-effacing!) No. You're the eldest, Susan whispers. Well, this is all very awkward, isn't it? The whole thing depends on getting to Aslan now before the witch gets here, and here they are stumbling about. Go on, Peter, go on. "We have come—Aslan" (p. 123). Now we all waited a beat, our hearts racing. What would happen? What would a lion's voice sound like? Our whole being was in our throats, our whole future passing in front of us.

"Welcome, Peter, Son of Adam. . . . Welcome, Susan and Lucy, Daughters of Eve. Welcome He-Beaver and She-Beaver" (p. 124). Oh my. His voice was so calming and gladdening. But he notices something, something quite obvious: "But where is the fourth?"

Yes, there are supposed to be four—four who will sit on thrones. Three is not enough. Three will not fulfill the prophecy. The fourth must be found. Who will explain? How can it be explained? Things have gone so badly, and now here is Aslan. How can we tell him? Mr. Beaver knows: just say it straight, Aslan wants the truth: "He has tried to betray them and join the White Witch" (p. 124). Well, so much for sugar-coating it! And then Peter felt obligated to say something and started to take some of the blame, but Aslan just listened and said nothing since there really was "nothing to be said." But Lucy, who once worried about whether Aslan was "safe," blurts out, "Please—Aslan . . . can anything be done to save Edmund?"

Whatever comes next, whatever Aslan says, one way or another, this is finally the point. *Can anything be done?* is the plea, and what Aslan says is the difference between life and death, not only for Edmund but for them all. The tension has built for hours, and now, here, it is at its peak. It's all on Aslan.

A HOPE IS STIRRED

"All shall be done. . . . But it may be harder than you think" (p. 124). And then silence for an unforgettable time; it was probably seconds, but it seemed like hours. For all of us Aslan no longer looked just royal, and majestic, and strong as a lion, which he was, but also suddenly a bit forlorn and sad. But just as quickly, Aslan "shook his mane and clapped his paws" and called for a feast to be prepared. And off went Lucy and Susan to work with the others, so Aslan can turn to Peter one-on-one to prepare him for what lay ahead. And what better way to instill confidence and courage than to point him to Cair Paravel, where he shall reign with his kin.

What a different scene compared with the way Edmund was offered a throne. Instead of appealing to Edmund's vanity, Aslan appeals to Peter's duty and honor as the firstborn and the high king, showing him the glories of Narnia. And as Peter was taking this all in, "a strange noise" interrupted his tender meditation. It was a horn. In fact, it was Susan's horn, declaring danger and need. And with Peter's sword drawn, Aslan commissions this once and future king to battle (p. 126). The witch's first wave has arrived.

And as he looked, he saw the naiads and dryads running in every direction and Lucy running toward him, and Susan climbing a tree to escape—what is that, a big dog? No, a wolf, the venerable Fenris Ulf himself! And Peter realized it was now or never—and off he rushed to save his sister with a mighty slash of his sword and missed him entirely. (Wolves are, shall we say, a bit harder and craftier to combat than mere men!) But the next blow would not be errant, and a quick thrust ended the threat as at the same time it portended more to come. Susan is safe! But the battle is now engaged, and Aslan sends forth his eagles and centaur to rescue Edmund and confront the queen! How, after so much travel and so little sleep, Peter was able to succeed, well, it's only by Aslan's hand, er, paw, that he made it. But this being his first battle, it's no wonder he forgot to clean his sword. And Aslan is there to commemorate and correct his swordsmanship and to confer knighthood upon him, this "Sir Peter Fenris-Bane" (p. 129). Wow.

What a scene, what a conquest. What victory must lay ahead! We hope! Aslan said this may be harder than we think, but so far it looks easy.

Deep Magic from the Dawn of Time (Chapter 13)

THRONES AND DETHRONING

This is where it gets good, right? Aslan, Peter, and all the rest of his entourage, Susan and Lucy included, stalk and dethrone the witch, rescue Edmund, and this sorry affair can come to a close and peace will reign in Narnia! Aslan the lion king is here, and all will be done and all will be well, he said so himself! Well, he did have that little asterisk about how it may be harder than we think, but how hard can that be? I mean, Peter has never used a sword in his life, and he just killed a wolf!

But there is more. There are those four thrones. And Cair Paravel. And then what to do with the queen who has usurped and ravaged and made stone statues of everyone who stood in her path. OK. Bring it on. What's next?

What's next is that the witch is not going down without a fight, and with the dwarf's suddenly sage counsel, she is going to play her trump card: Edmund. After all that walking, Edmund's ready for a resolution too. Or so he thinks. What will become of Edmund? The dwarf, who knows Aslan probably has a plan too, and offers the best diversion he can come up with: make Edmund a hostage! A bargaining chip. The whole point is to keep the thrones unoccupied after all. The prophecy says four sons and daughters of Adam and Eve, and so even if the three are crowned, Edmund's absence will prevent her overthrow. While Aslan is preoccupied with Edmund, they can dispense with the rest!

Edmund will be taken to the stone table. (It still sounds ominous.) And the witch is not too revealing of what will take place there: "I would like to have done it on the Stone Table itself," she says (p. 131). Have what done? What is the "it" that will be done?

Why is it "the proper place"? What does it mean when she says, "That is where it has always been done before?" (p. 131). Why it's enough to make a grown man or boy cry! Whatever "it" is, Edmund doesn't like the sound of "it"!

Preparation must be made. And it looks like Aslan and company have made it a bit easier on them by showing up at the stone table already! But the news is still a bit startling: somehow, someway, she learns, her captain, the wolf, Fenris Ulf, has been killed by one of the sons of Adam! The queen is flabbergasted. But then they have been with "him," with Aslan, and that explains enough; so there's no time to waste. All the nasties of Narnia must be summoned, from ghouls to hags, and ogres to spectres—the cream of the crop of her minions. And while they're off to no good, she's got her own chores—preparing Edmund for (gulp!) sacrifice on the stone table! Bound with his back against a tree, he hears a horrific sound, a *whizz whizz whizz* (p. 133).

It sounds like, uh, something being sharpened. Oh no, that knife isn't for a grand dinner buffet. It's for *him*. Oh, this is horrible. Can't Aslan do something? What's that noise, that conversation, that buzz? Maybe, yes, could it be that Aslan's army has attacked! Something's happened, and Edmund can't tell what it is. "Who's got the witch?" someone says. Another: "Do you mean she's escaped?" And, "What's that? Oh sorry it's only an old stump" (p. 134). Edmund wasn't sure, of course, but it sounded like somebody had come upon the witch and her crew and had, maybe, come to rescue Edmund? Of course, Edmund would never know for sure what happened because by the time Aslan's rescue team, led by the centaurs and unicorns and deer and birds, arrived, he'd fainted! But that crafty old witch and her dwarf accomplice had by magic disguised themselves as a stump and a boulder! They could remain hidden in plain sight for as long as her spell could be sustained.

When the children wake up in their camp near the pavilion and the stone table, they learn that, hurrah, Edmund has been secured and was now in the company of Aslan. And as they looked, they saw the two of them, walking together, their conversation a secret, of course, but one which Edmund could never ever forget. Whatever it was and however he came to grips with what he'd done, he'd now begun to apologize and shake hands with everyone. It is so hard to know how to ask for forgiveness and equally hard to know how to accept an apology. The fact that the children might find it awkward is no surprise, but before too much awkwardness came, one of Aslan's citizens, a leopard, carries forth the queen's message—a request from her dwarf for safe passage so she could discuss a matter "as much to [his] advantage as to hers" (p. 136).

What this could possibly be, of course, given the vain and murderous foolishness of the witch, is unimaginable. Aslan the king and lord of Narnia needing to discuss with the self-appointed queen a matter of advantage to him? Preposterous. Even Mr. Beaver is offended; what right does she even have to the title of queen? But Aslan assures "all names will soon be restored to their proper owners" (p. 137). Indeed they will, indeed they will. Why, we will just ambush this queen and . . . wait a minute, why Aslan is going along with it—he *is* granting her safe passage, and he will "negotiate" with her! What is he thinking? His ways are not our ways.

DEEP MAGIC

For a while the three children who had not seen the witch before were transfixed. A witch! And as they watched the animated conversation between the witch and Aslan unfold, they became more and more frightened, not of her so much as what might have to be done to defeat her. "You have a traitor there, Aslan," the witch—as prosecutor and executioner—boldly states (p. 138). What's it to you? Aslan more or less tells her. "Have you forgotten the Deep Magic?" the witch asks. Hmmm. *Deep magic.* Sounds important. Is it like the magic in the wardrobe? Like the magic in the witch's bottle? Like the magic that turns living creatures to stone? What is this "Deep Magic"? *Does* Aslan know about it? Of course, he does. He's Aslan.

But he will play along: "Let us say I have forgotten it." And then the queen goes into what sounds like a chronological history of the Deep Magic. What is that she said? How mysterious! That it is written on the stone table? That it is written in deep letters on a trunk of the world ash trees? That it is engraved on the scepter of the Emperor-Beyond-the-Sea? That he, the emperor, put this Deep Magic into Narnia at the very beginning?

Whoa. This sounds a little like that Lilith stuff we learned about earlier, only it's not about our world; it's about Narnia. Narnia's ancient and mystery-laden history. It's just not clear what this Deep Magic is. And who the emperor is. And how any of it is relevant to Edmund's fate and what Aslan is going to do about it. But then it gets clearer when she states it plainly: "You know that every traitor belongs to me as my lawful prey and that for every treachery I have a right to a kill" (p. 139). Whatever that means, we know it means Edmund is the traitor. We just hope Aslan has as good a command of history and this Deep Magic as she does! Surely, he knows a loophole! Otherwise, it looks like things could get out of hand. But there doesn't seem to be any reason we cannot overpower the queen, take her wand, and be done with. Why, look at the bull with the man's head, and those centaurs and eagles and leopards are not to be toyed with. We've got the numbers.

But it's not going to be that easy. You can tell from Aslan that he is not going to win Edmund's ransom with violence. He is actually listening to the witch's argument, and, worse, seems to be accepting it! When it looks like the bull will stage a battle, the witch reacts:

> "Fool," said the Witch with a savage smile . . . "do you really think your master can rob me of my rights by mere force? He knows the Deep Magic better than that. He knows that unless I have blood as the Law says all Narnia will be overturned and perish in fire and water" (p. 139).

Oh my! Speak, Aslan, speak. Tell her she's wrong; tell her there's another way. Tell her she's got no claim on him since she seduced him in the first place! But that's not what Aslan says. "It is very true," said Aslan, "I do not deny it" (p. 139). Oh, no! Oh, no! It's worse than we could ever have imagined! Could it be that the deceitful, conniving, treacherous witch has the law on her side!

Susan, Lucy, Peter—we're all beside ourselves now! This can't be! We've come this far; this can't be the end of the story. You can't be bargaining for Edmund's life with the witch. Then Susan says what we are all thinking, "Can't we do something about the Deep Magic? Isn't there something you can work against it?" (p. 139). What and how Aslan answers is something none of us would ever forget: "Work against the Emperor's magic?" (p. 140). Clearly that is not an option. Whoever this emperor is, he clearly has more authority and power than Aslan. There is nothing else to be done. The Deep Magic is the Deep Magic after all. That means it's the law. All had been said publicly that was going to be said. Aslan would now talk to the witch alone. What seemed like hours passed, and then Aslan finally spoke. "I have settled the matter. She has renounced all claims on your brother's blood" (p. 141). Relief. We could breathe again. Joy. But wait.

And what seemed like relief was transformed into further anxiety when the witch cries out, "But how do I know this promise will be kept?" (p. 141). What promise? We thought it was the end of the matter. What else needs to be done? Edmund is safe. The witch is retreating. The day is ending with joy. What promise? And then Aslan's roar tells us that something is still awry, and when the queen "ran for her life" (p. 141), we became worried. What in the world is going on? Aslan? Aslan? What's the story? This is all very disconcerting! Is it over, or not?

Reflecting on the Journey So Far

Some visitors to Narnia may begin to get a bit confused, along with Susan, with the turn the story takes when Aslan and the white witch begin to debate the merits of the Deep Magic. "Why," we might ask, as Susan in effect herself does, "Why can we not just forget the Deep Magic or avoid the consequences and just save Edmund." We are told that Aslan growls and everyone gets the point. What is the story behind the Deep Magic? To disobey the law that punishes traitors and betrayers—to seek to undermine its power to order and to regulate Narnian society—would be disastrous. For then there would truly be no rule of law, no standards of justice, no way even to bring the witch to trial. It would end Narnia just as the witch says from a judgment by the Emperor-Beyond-the-Sea. For no lawless society can continue to exist and can only wax more evil over time.

We need to see that though the white witch manipulates the law, the law itself is good. Without this provision, "traitorhood" would be honored; and all manner of deceit, conspiracy, and backstabbing would be essential character traits in Narnian culture. (Something equally awful, immoral, and treacherous—the institution of slavery—does emerge in the land of Calormen, as told in the tale *The Horse and His Boy,* and we are thus shown graphically the consequences of following someone other than Aslan, and a law founded on something other than his truthful and righteous character.)

This is why Aslan speaks so calmly and forthrightly in this scene. He will not practice the same deceit and cunning as the witch. When he suggests, "Let us say I have forgotten" (about the Deep Magic), he is inviting the witch to do something she does not know how to do: to argue, rationally, for the superiority of the position she is advocating. The killing of a traitor based on the evidence. But she is not interested in justice and has no desire to uphold Narnian character. From the beginning her motives were self-preservation and the accumulation of total power. She thought, mistakenly, supremely ironically, that as judge and executioner, she could somehow parlay Edmund's death into preventing the calamity of losing her own throne.

But the queen is not clever enough to have thought beyond the death of Edmund, and certainly she has no ulterior plan to dethrone or kill Aslan—whose very name makes her cringe. Aslan willingly lays down his life; she cannot take it from him. She can't think beyond the moment, and she would not have even gotten this far without her dwarf's help. The truth is, the white witch has no imagination and certainly no inkling of the true purpose of Deep Magic, no knowledge or empathy that would permit her to envision Aslan choosing to lay down his life for another—and thereby saving not only Edmund, but Narnia itself, all in obedience to his father, the great Emperor-Beyond-the-Sea. She cannot conceive of a person who willingly acts on behalf of another, willing to divest himself of his power and authority so that a higher purpose and higher calling can be achieved. She has never known a selfless act. When we read *The Magician's Nephew,* we find out why.

Our own impulse is either to lash out and win the day with aggression and violence or to run from danger and to avoid conflict by finding a compromise—a way around the Deep Magic, so to speak. But notice the noble qualities of each of the characters who has dedicated his or her life to defeating the evil white witch. The Beavers have especially, from first to last, been witnesses to Aslan's justice and have remained loyal to the Pevensies, housing, feeding, educating, and guiding them. Even in this scene of turmoil and gravity, the beavers stand tall in their integrity and their faith. They may not completely understand what is going on before them, but they do understand the witch, and their righteous indignation, rather than cowering fear, is impressive and inspiring. They stand their ground. And they obey Aslan.

Some Background Notes

FATHER CHRISTMAS

Father Christmas, or Santa Claus, is of course a familiar figure and perhaps a strange one to show up in Narnia. Father Christmas himself is a son of Adam, and how he "got in" and how he fits into Narnia's celebration of Christmas is not explored by the narrator of the story. What is not mysterious is Lewis's love of mixing mythologies. The Christian story of Christ's incarnation and the celebration called Christmas do not entirely mesh with the unfolding storyline in Narnia, but, from Lewis's point of view, there is no reason he should not appear to signal the coming of Aslan and the beginning of the thaw. He is there to bring gifts that will bless and equip the children for their adventure and is meant to bring them joy and hope. For the Beavers and other Narnians, he clearly is a familiar figure that they too associate with Aslan's coming. So, symbolically, Father Christmas serves as a kind of messenger in both worlds, bearing the same message. The coming of God's Son, and the coming of the son of the Emperor-Beyond-the-Sea, should be celebrated because he himself is the best gift of all. It does not occur to Lewis that Father Christmas has somehow to play the same role in Narnia that he plays on the other side of the wardrobe. It's not an allegory, he would chide us.

STONE TABLE

The stone table has here a number of resonances. First, it reminds us of the tablets of stone on which God wrote the Ten Commandments delivered to Moses for the people of Israel in the book of Exodus. The witch points out that the Deep Magic she wishes to wield to gain her prey is written on the stone table. Second, it reminds of the altars on which sacrifices were made in the Old Testament Scriptures, and which further points in the New Testament Scriptures to the story of Jesus' death on the cross, a sacrifice which atones for the sin of the whole world. In the next chapter we will see this for ourselves in the heroism of Aslan.

DEEP MAGIC

The Deep Magic is something the queen has surprisingly memorized, but it is utterly unlike any of the magic she wields in her dastardly reign. The Deep Magic does not originate with her, but with the Emperor-Beyond-the-Sea. And whoever the emperor is, both she and Aslan recognize his authority to announce and enforce the Deep Magic. Simply put, it represents a law that requires death for those who betray anyone in Narnia—a "life for a life," so to speak. It is central to being a citizen of Narnia—respect for others and honoring their right to life. Its positive parallel is, "Do unto others as you would have others do unto you." Sometimes called the Golden Rule, it is from the teaching of Jesus (Luke 6:31). The irony is that this scoundrel of a queen is, of course, guilty herself of violating the Deep Magic and is complicit in Edmund's own traitorous behavior. But the irony is lost on her, and her kingdom is also about to be lost to her, in the kind of cosmic irony that Tolkien called "the eucatastrophe" (as we explained in chapter 1). The very means by which she seeks to secure her throne is the source of her downfall.

Chapter 6

Deep Magic Is Never Enough:

The Lion, the Witch and the Wardrobe, Chapters 14–17

The pace is quickening each moment. In fact, the pace is almost intolerable. Since all of us came through the wardrobe, hoping to save Mr. Tumnus, the stakes have steadily risen. With the defection of Edmund, we have been both the hunters and the hunted. Through it all, the hope of meeting Aslan and the promise that he might save our fallen comrade Mr. Tumnus, rescue Edmund, and free Narnia has been our single vision and motivation. Mr. Beaver knew what he meant when he said that Aslan was "not safe but good." One surprise after another.

Who knew that once we met up with Aslan we would so quickly meet up with the witch too? The likely outcomes seem to have dwindled to a handful. Edmund is free and safe, but something else seems still to be under the witch's control. Aslan clearly has superior strength and has the witch and her crew doing his bidding. But something is not quite right. And who is this Emperor-Beyond-the-Sea, anyway? Enough speculating, and enough waiting. The climax beckons, and we must see all things through to their end.

The Triumph of the Witch (Chapter 14)

A LONELY VIGIL

We were all biting our tongues, wondering whether we could get up the courage to ask Aslan what was said between him and the witch. But he wasn't sharing. As Aslan told us to break camp and then prepared us for the final campaign against the witch, we talked among ourselves about what might lay ahead. We had long ago stopped wondering what was happening in the professor's house or in London and how our parents were. In the heat of our own battles and intrigues, we had forgotten all about the world of Adam and Eve and had become more and more accustomed to thinking like Narnians think. Which only means thinking like the beavers, and like Aslan, because they have been our mentors and exemplars. They inspire courage, loyalty, and trust. Whatever we were before we got here, we will never be the same again. Even Edmund has changed.

Looks like Peter is getting most of the attention from Aslan. They are going over strategies for the witch's inevitable retreat under siege. Two plans, one for the woods and one for the castle, were in place, but then something occurred to Peter as he and Aslan discussed them. Peter wondered why Aslan would tell him these things since surely he would be there too, but Aslan's abrupt answer, "I can give you no promise of that," told Peter and through him told us all something we did not want to contemplate or divulge by coming right out and saying it. Aslan is doing something else. Something he and he alone will do.

It wasn't at all clear why we had moved from the stone table and the pavilion when we did and why we moved our camp out here. It seemed to make us somehow more vulnerable. But Aslan dismissed all these worries and frankly seemed distracted—there won't be a "night attack," he said, but we didn't know why. It was almost as if Aslan knew exactly when and where the witch would strike and that it would not be worth our worry to strategize. He would somehow take care of it. Alone. The "good times" that seemed to lay before all of us now suddenly seemed a distant memory. Aslan's mood affected all of us (p. 144).

And what was that mood exactly? Something like resignation. Something like sadness. Something like dread. And Lucy and Susan both picked up on it and could not sleep? Who could? But it wasn't fear of the witch and her henchmen anymore but fear of losing Aslan so soon after he found us. And so off they went to look for Aslan, as much to comfort themselves as him. But as they sought him, they noticed him walking off slowly in the direction of the stone table (it still sounds ominous!). And so they followed, and in the pale moonlight Aslan looked different: "His head and tail hung low and he walked slowly as if he were very, very tired" (p. 146). And then he realized he was being trailed: "Oh, children, children, why are you following me?" (p. 146).

They wanted so to follow him and keep him company this night of all nights, and he acquiesced, though they had to promise to stop when he said. Their hearts were breaking each step of the way, for though they said nothing, deep within they had an inkling of what was about to happen. They begged him to tell, if it would have helped him to tell, but he simply told them to be careful to hide and not to be seen once what was going to happen commenced. What was going to happen? The time had come for him to leave them behind.

THE WORK OF THE STONE TABLE

They could not believe what they were seeing. Such horrible creatures! Creatures whose very species make one cringe: Incubuses, Wraiths, Afreets, Sprites, Wooses . . . all on the witch's side, spectators to what would be the awfulest of deeds. An innocent and sinless lion would be killed. Instead of another. She cannot control her glee: "The fool!" she cried. "The fool has come. Bind him fast" (p. 149). The fool? She cannot believe that Aslan has come willingly, and he has come to take the place of Edmund. That is the awful, terrible bargain he had reached with the witch. And oh the indignities this great and magnificent lion had to endure, offering no resistance! They dragged him and cut off his mane and mocked him and jeered at him like the scoundrels and lowlifes they were: "Why, he's only a great cat after all." "Puss, Puss! Poor Pussy!" "Would you like a saucer of milk, Pussums?" (p. 150).

Oh my oh my. His shorn face looked never so noble—and here, in Lucy's eyes, he was "more beautiful and more patient than ever" (p. 151). Muzzled, then dragged to the table, their nefarious deeds were about to be finished, but not without one more round of kicking and hitting and spitting. Poor Aslan! Poor Narnia! Poor Edmund! Poor us! And the queen did her dirty work, baring her arms and raising then the knife that looked like stone and bore a strange and evil shape. Time for one more speech. (Aren't the villainous always so chatty and talkative and proud of their terrible deeds?)

> And now, who has won? Fool, did you think that by all this you would save the human traitor? Now I will kill you instead of him as our pact was and so the Deep Magic will be appeased. . . . Understand that you have given me Narnia forever, you have lost your own life and you have not saved his. In that knowledge, despair and die (p. 152).

We covered our eyes. We could not bear to see this happen. Is there no justice? Is there no one to hear our heart cry? Is this the end of Aslan, and of all of us, and of Narnia? Who will answer her treachery? As long as we have breath, we refuse to "despair and die." We must tell the others.

Deeper Magic from Before the Dawn of Time (Chapter 15)

SURPRISE, SURPRISE!

Sometimes our wishes come true beyond what we could ever think, or ask, or imagine. If we only had perspective, we might be able to see that our prayers are always answered too, but in surprising and startling ways. In Narnia, when all seemed lost, when it seemed that the wicked had triumphed, when our hearts were broken, well, there were still a few surprises left, which, if we knew only the Deep Magic, we could never have guessed. The Deep Magic teaches Narnians how to be good Narnians and marks anti-Narnian behavior as it is: evil, treacherous, traitorous. To obey the Deep Magic is to practice loving one's neighbor as oneself.

Which is something the queen could never do. Love was a foreign concept. And that is why when she finished killing Aslan, she was keen to finish us off. And away she went with her legions of ghouls and minotaurs and spectres, seeking to end the rebellion against her and to fill Narnia with stone statues. And as they departed, looking for Aslan's remnant, Lucy and Susan crept down to the stone table to unmuzzle and untie their beloved Aslan. And they would have help! Even the mice of the fields would come to nibble away his bonds, even as Lucy and Susan were gently embracing him.

Without the ropes and the muzzle, Aslan seemed more like himself. As the light of morning grew, and the birds began to sang, their hearts were lifted; and they decided to walk a bit, trying to keep warm as they witnessed the sun rising, spotting Cair Paravel against a red and golden line where the sea met the sky. And then they heard the crack! And in their tender state, they could only think that something awful had just happened—again.

The rising sun made everything different, and they could not be sure, as they ran back to the stone table, whether they could trust their eyes. The stone table looked broken in two, and Aslan was missing. What could have happened? More enemies? More magic? "Yes. . . . It is more magic" a great voice behind them called out (p. 159). And you could not have imagined or anticipated who it was who was speaking . . . Aslan! Aslan has come back, shining in the sun, shaking his mane, as if he had never died!

How could this be? How could this wonderful thing have happened when all looked lost and Aslan lay dead? Tell us, Aslan, tell us! They could not help but shower him with hugs and kisses! You're not a ghost, are you? You really, really are here, and all will be well? Tell us, Aslan!

The Deeper Magic

Yes. Aslan is back. Yes, Aslan is real! You see, there is something more than Deep Magic. Something stronger than death. Something mightier than evil. Oh, Aslan, tell us what this means:

"It means," said Aslan, "that though the Witch knew the Deep Magic, there is a magic deeper still which she did not know. Her knowledge goes back only to the dawn of Time. But if she could have looked a little further back . . . she would have read a different incantation. She would have known that when a willing victim who had committed no treachery was killed in a traitor's stead, the Table would crack and Death itself would start working backwards. And now—"

Aslan's "and now" was the richest, most wonderful, most exhilarating pause they had ever experienced—and the anticipation grew for what would come after the "now"! His strength has returned! He wanted to romp like a lion and roar like a lion! And for some time he leaped, and they chased, and they rolled over; and for the first time in many, many years, someone in Narnia was merely playing. Playing! Oh, what it means to be so free of care and so free of heart and spirit that one can play, enjoy, and be recreated in the moment of self-forgetfulness.

But there was business yet to finish and no time to reflect on what he meant by the deeper magic. That would have to come later, after dealing with the queen. And so there was nothing to do but climb on Aslan's back and allow him to carry them back to the scene of battle, to the witch's house. What a ride, a ride that carried them through one amazing sight after another as the glory of a resurrection morning burst forth, and all of nature was alive with the promise and the reality of a new life. And oh that final leap over the castle wall—our hearts in our throats and our stomachs, well, let's not talk about that. Clinging to dear life, clinging to Aslan, who is our Dear Life, we flew over the wall, tumbling off into the courtyard of statues.

What Happened about the Statues (Chapter 16)

THE BREATH OF LIFE

Well, it looked like a museum, a ghastly museum. But, hush, Aslan is on the move. He was moving from statue to statue, starting with the stone lion, breathing on them, and with each breath they came to life. Everyone who had been frozen mid-action, caught in a stone spell from the witch's magic wand, was freed from their stiff, stationary pose and brought out of their death-sleep and into life, into Narnia, into the presence of Aslan. How glorious this resurrection scene! Aslan is first, and then the rest. He is risen, is alive, and brings the gift of life to those who had fallen prey to the witch. The sight of the stone coming back to life was emblematic of everyone's transformation: "For a second after Aslan breathed upon him the stone lion looked just the same. Then a tiny streak of gold began to run along his white marble back—then it spread—then the color seemed to lick all over him as flame licks all over a piece of paper."

Life spread. Aslan's life had begun to be spread all around. It could not be stopped. Narnians, talking beasts, and creatures of all kinds were "roaring, braying, yelping, barking, stamping," the shouts and hurrahs and songs and laughter were irrepressible! (p. 166). Life cannot be squelched. The spirit cannot be quenched. *Life*! Aslan's life! His resurrected life freely given to those whose lives had been taken by the witch. Even the giant revived, feet first: "Bless me! I must have been asleep. Now! Where's that dratted little Witch that's running about on the ground. Somewhere just by my feet it was" (p. 167). Yes, where was this witch, this murderous queen, so destructive and so wicked? It is time to deal with her.

THE QUEEN'S DEMISE

I know what you are thinking. And so was Lucy. Where is Mr. Tumnus? Our friend the faun with whom this whole adventure on the other side of the wardrobe began. We must find him. Where could he be? We need Aslan to breathe upon him and bring him life. As they ransack the witch's house, Lucy discovers him. "Aslan! Aslan! I've found Mr. Tumnus. Oh, do come quick!" (p. 168). Ah, yes, back to life, and what stories to tell! But there is still this story to bring to closure. We must find that witch. Aslan can just bound over the wall again, and we are stuck in the locked-up courtyard. (Neither Father Christmas nor Aslan need to worry about locked doors!) How do we get out?

Oh, yeah, the giant. And his giant club. It's for Aslan to ask for his help—and help he does, swinging that club and knocking down the gates with his third blow and the towers with a fourth. And then with a spontaneous reunion sort of erupting, Lucy and Tumnus get better acquainted with the giant, Mr. Rumblebuffin. Family histories! But,

Aslan reminds, there's work to do! A battle to be enjoined. The whole courtyard had become Aslan's battalion.

At the lions' gait (Aslan and his newly refreshed lion comrade, who loves Aslan because there's no "standoffishness" in him), the army moves swiftly and surely to the narrow valley where Peter and Edmund were in desperate straits, fending off the witch's army. And, oh, the painful sight of seeing more statues arrayed on the field of battle—the witch's wand still at work. And if you looked even more closely—it was Peter fighting the witch straight on! But she had not her wand, only a dagger, and Peter his sword! How will it end? For clearly, this is the most important engagement of all!

And end it would—"Off my back, children!" shouted Aslan, and "with a roar that shook all Narnia" he flung himself upon the white witch (p. 174). Lucy looked on with "horror and amazement," as Aslan and the witch tumbled, and he rolled over her, finishing her off, as his army of centaurs and unicorns and the giant and all the liberated creatures from the witch's courtyard "rushed madly on the enemy's line," completing their mission (p. 174).

Free at last, free at last, Narnia is free at last.

The Hunting of the White Stag (Chapter 17)

THE TOLL

The remaining battle did not take long with Aslan at the helm. Most of the enemy had been vanquished with the first charge. Those aligned with her, who saw the witch fall, either surrendered or ran away. It was time to take stock. What a sight to see Peter and Aslan shaking hands. And Lucy noticed that Peter now looked older—and wiser. Battle will do that. For war has its costs.

"It was all Edmund's doing, Aslan," Peter explained. "We'd have been beaten if it hadn't been for him" (p. 175). Where *was* Edmund? That's a question the Pevensies had been asking themselves most of this journey. Oh, no! he's been terribly wounded, thrashing the witch's hand to break her wand. It was the turning point. But can anything be done for Edmund? Mrs. Beaver has him and, oh my, the blood, and his face is so green!

Aslan knew what to do. "Quick, Lucy," he said. And Lucy remembered Father Christmas's gift of the cordial that would heal Edmund. What a great Christmas gift that turned out to be, saving Edmund's life. And suddenly Aslan helped her realize that there were other wounded and that this Christmas gift was like the first one, and it too was given to all to provide life. And then it was time to rest from their battles. And to be grateful for all that was done for them, by Aslan, by the Beavers, by all the Narnians who for so long had been waiting for the sons of Adam and the daughters of Eve to come.

When you have heard the stories all your life, and then they finally do come true, it is an amazing feeling. To witness the real story coming to life that had only been a dream or a prophecy, or a wish—it is awesome and beyond words. That was how it felt to the Narnians. For the Pevensie clan, it must have felt much different because they had come, seemingly, as accidental intruders, and the more they talked, and the more time they spent with Aslan, they realized that it had been no accident for them to be in Narnia, and that, in fact, it had been their destiny to fill the four thrones at Cair Paravel.

And the day after their day of rest, they indeed celebrated a coronation at the great hall of Cair Paravel. The cries of "Long live King Peter! Long live Queen Susan! Long live King Edmund! Long live Queen Lucy!" lived on in their memories long after they had been shouted out by the citizens of Narnia. And here the adventure seemed to be on fast forward, as the sons and daughters of Adam and Eve assumed their roles as royalty in the kingdom, and Aslan had quietly slipped away.

Somehow this did not disturb or alarm them, for Mr. Beaver himself had told them that "he doesn't like being tied down—and of course he has other countries to attend to. It's quite all right. He'll often drop in. Only you mustn't press him. He's wild, you know. Not like a *tame* lion" (p. 180). No, indeed, he is not a tame lion, as all of Narnia, including the witch, and the Pevensies learned. Not tame. Not safe. But good.

THE REST OF THE STORY

Well, it would seem like this is where one would say, "And they lived happily ever after," and, in a way, this certainly applies. Because the kings and queens of Narnia ruled well, finishing off the remnants of the queen's army that had fled, making good laws that preserved the peace, making Narnia's borders secure with good treaties and growing in stature and grace and joy. All of Narnia shared this joy and enjoyed this peace. And in enjoying their bounty and their joy, they had time for recreation, including the hunting of the white stag who, if caught, would grant wishes.

By now the Pevensies had long forgotten their homeland's speech (and, let's be frank, most if not all of their former life as young Londoners) and spoke with an elevated and courtly tone, "Fair Consorts, let us now alight from our horses and follow this beast into the thicket, for in all my days I never hunted a nobler quarry," said King Peter (p. 182).

And you know now how it is in Narnia. One thing leads to another, and as they chase the white stag, they move from one woods to another, and, lo and behold, they come upon what you and I know is a lamppost. None of them can remember exactly why or how, but this lamppost looks familiar. Who knows how long they have been on this side of the wardrobe? How many years have passed? The hunt for the white stag must cease, and the four of them will embark, in the name of Aslan, on this new adventure, for they must discover the significance of this lamppost.

And so they leave behind their horses and set out through the thicket, branch after branch, until it is not branches they are passing through but, what's this: fur! Fur coats? And this is the wardrobe they had left so long ago! Oh, my! "And the next moment they came tumbling out of a wardrobe door into the empty room, and they were no longer Kings and Queens in their hunting array but just Peter, Susan, Edmund, and Lucy in their own clothes" (p. 185).

Oh my, is that Mrs. Macready's voice we hear? We are back. We groan. It must be the very same day we fled the tourists and hid in the wardrobe. They would be lucky that none of them ever came into that room. They must now find the professor and explain why the coats were missing. What would he say? And would he laugh at them or think them silly or crazy?

Of course not. The professor knows more than he has told us before. But how could he unless . . . . What is that he says? We can't get back to Narnia through the wardrobe again? How sad. But wait, that sounds good: "Once a King or Queen of Narnia, always a King or Queen in Narnia!" But, we protest, if we can go back, tell us how we can get back? How do we get there? He puts us off. Don't try to get there at all, he says, and don't talk to people about it unless you know they've been to Narnia. But how should we know that? we plead. "Oh, you'll *know* all right. Odd things they say—even their looks—will let the secret out. Keep your eyes open. Bless me, what *do* they teach them at these schools?" (p. 186).

Why the professor sounds like he knows a lot about Narnia. Almost as if he has been there himself. But how could that be? We just have to ask him more questions.

Reflecting on the Journey's End

As every Narnian visitor learns, in order to come back, we must first leave, and we will never return through the same entryway again. Once through the wardrobe, we need to find a new way in—and, happily, Aslan supplies it, but only in his way and for his purposes.

The good news as we return to our world is that as we exit the wardrobe, our Narnian adventures are just getting started. Literally we can return to Narnia, and it will be through a different portal each time. There is, literally, a sequel, *Prince Caspian*, that follows the return of the Pevensies to the land of Narnia many years later as they rescue a king to be and a kingdom from a new enemy. And then there is a sequel to that one, called *The Voyage of the Dawn Treader*, that picks up where that one leaves off, an exciting sea escapade with now King Caspian on a follow-up mission from Aslan. And, believe it or not, then there is a sequel to that one, too, called *The Silver Chair*, that traces a new set of heroes who must, once again, restore order to Narnia, helping Caspian's son, Prince Rilian, gain the throne that he has been prevented from ascending by evil enchantment.

These form what some Narnian scholars have called a "Caspian triad," since in one way or another they provide a continuous narrative involving a discrete era in the history of Narnia.

The three tales that follow these are more diverse and portray some unique settings. *The Horse and His Boy* takes us to a new and unexplored geographical region: Calormen, which we have heard about if we have read *The Voyage of the Dawn Treader*, but it is a much different landscape, set in an Arabian-style southern desert land, featuring a young man and a young woman trying to escape their not-so-glorious futures by finding meaning in their past, and who are helped (and hindered) by two talking horses from Narnia. *The Magician's Nephew*, which we talked about in the introduction, tells the story of how Narnia came into being through the Song of Aslan, and how Digory Kirke became the professor of the very first Narnian tale. Finally, *The Last Battle*, whence the title of this book comes, gives us the final story of how Narnia is saved once more by Aslan in a grand reunion of all our favorite human and Narnian characters.

We have gone "further up and further in" during our exploration of *The Lion, the Witch and the Wardrobe* in order to experience the further joy of seeing not only the lines themselves but what is between them. We have wanted to look along, and not just look at, Narnia. We have wanted an indigenous journey, seeing through the eyes of those who live and move and have their being in Narnia, not as outsiders but as insiders. And that is what the Old and New Testaments are to be to us: true stories, told by insiders, whose lives and whose words were ordained by God to instruct, inspire, and redeem. The more time we spend inhabiting the world of Jesus in the power of the Holy Spirit, the more we are equipped to live in our world, in the present, as we look to the future.

The testimony of many readers of Narnia is that C. S. Lewis has not just identified a longing or God-shaped vacuum already there; he has helped create the longing itself. In experiencing Narnia, we are led to confess that we are all displaced persons, expatriates, exiles. And there is a longing deep, deep within us; there is a call resonating in our innermost being for home, for the smells, sounds, caresses, and comforts that we only dimly recall; a call tells us that we were made for eternity, that our identity and purpose and destiny originate elsewhere, not on this fallen planet and not within our own limited imaginations. Lewis captures it so well here:

Most of us find it very difficult to want "Heaven" at all— except in so far as "Heaven" means meeting again our friends who have died. One reason for this difficulty is that we have not been trained: our whole education tends to fix our minds on this world. Another reason is that when the real want for Heaven is present in us, we do not recognize it. Most people, if they had really learned to look into their own hearts, would know that they do want, and want acutely, something that cannot be had in this world. There are all sorts of things in this world that offer to give it to you, but they never quite keep their promise. The longings which arise in us when we first fall in love, or first think of some foreign country, or first take up some subject that excites us, are longings which no marriage, no travel, no learning, can really satisfy.[1]

Yes, that's it, that's what Narnia helps us see. That our longing points us home, and that this is not our home. Only heaven can satisfy our deepest longing. Narnia trains us to be pilgrims and to look forward to that homecoming that awaits us. To find our compass, and our counsel, in the word of Aslan, which is the Word of God. Kings and queens, sons of Adam and daughters of Eve, we shall be. Aslan has prepared many mansions for us. And we will reign with him.

Some Background Notes

DEEPER MAGIC FROM BEFORE THE DAWN OF TIME

As Aslan's sacrifice proves, there is something older, something wiser, something deeper than the Deep Magic, which is, as we have noted, essentially the law. This law is what regulates justice, keeps order, provides the criteria for maintaining character and growth in one's own life. It comes from the Emperor-Beyond-the-Sea, who is Aslan's father, and to whom he is committed. The law is good, but it is not supreme. There is a higher law, and that is the law of love—the law of grace and mercy—and that is what the deeper magic is: the willingness of an innocent victim to die in the place of another. It is important to note that this deeper magic is "from Before the Dawn of Time." The witch knows the Deep Magic—the law or principle that regulates Narnia. But she seems ignorant of the fact that something might have existed "before Narnia," and that the origins of Narnia come from somewhere deeper and further back in time. Her ignorance, her lack of curiosity of what may lay behind Narnia, is her downfall. She is a materialist—a witch—whose life and identity and "spells" emanate from a temporal point of view. She manipulates what "is," but she cannot create "ex nihilo" (out of nothing). But Aslan comes from over the sea—like his father the emperor. And, as we learn in *The Magician's Nephew,* he created Narnia, sang her into being. It simply does not occur to her that there may be a deeper magic. Aslan's deeper magic, his love, and his grace and mercy, are unknown to her. But they are mighty and powerful and "save to the uttermost those who are being saved" (Heb. 7:25).

Not a Tame Lion

Mr. Beaver's words here capture the essence of Aslan's character and identity. Aslan cannot be domesticated. He cannot be trapped against his will. He is the son of the Emperor-Beyond-the-Sea. He lays down his life, so no one takes it from him (John 10:17–19). There is a freedom then that gives Aslan his authority, and an authority that gives Aslan his freedom. He must not and cannot disobey the Deep Magic, for that would be an affront to his Father, and thus a violation of his eternal law. Aslan cannot deny himself. To do so would be to undermine the very kingship that he is seeking to assert. No, he must willingly submit in obedience to his Father and by that obedience will win the day. Aslan's story, like Christ's, is one of playing by the rules, rules he himself has ordained in order to provide righteousness and justice. In the end, in order to save Edmund and Narnia, he is willing to lay down his life and thereby may take it up again under his Father's loving embrace. The picture of Aslan breathing life into the stone statues is thus a picture of our new life in Christ as he forgives us and resurrects us out of the death of our old selves. He is not a tame lion, he is not a safe lion, but he is good, and in that goodness brings us back from the dead to live again to pursue a godly life.

GRACE

The New Testament theme of grace is at work in this tale. *Grace* means "unmerited favor or care." In this case Aslan's willing sacrifice on behalf of Edmund not only rescues Edmund but also brings Narnia back to its rightful order. Grace operates without strings and is a free gift of the one who bestows it. Edmund is not saved because he deserves it but because Aslan wills it.

REDEMPTION

This concept, which has primary roots in the Bible but also in many ancient traditions, focuses on the character's transformation over the course of a story. In this case Edmund's character is both thematically and literally "redeemed." He both grows and matures during his adventures, regretting his evil and embracing the good, and is also redeemed by Aslan's sacrifice, making it possible for him to escape the consequences of his deeds by Aslan's virtues, not his own.

RESURRECTION

Lewis uses the New Testament story of Christ's resurrection from the dead as the basis for Aslan's return to life. The Emperor-Beyond-the-Sea brings his son, the great lion, back from the dead. Without Aslan, Narnia will die.

RESTORATION

After the white witch and her followers are defeated, order can be restored to Narnia and its rightful rulers established—in this case, Peter, Susan, Lucy, and Edmund. This is in fulfillment of the prophecy that two sons of Adam and two daughters of Eve would reign in Narnia.

For Further Reading

Baehr, Ted, and James Baehr. *Narnia Beckons: C. S. Lewis's The Lion, the Witch and the Wardrobe and Beyond*. Nashville: Broadman & Holman, 2005.

Carnell, Corbin S. *Bright Shadow of Reality: Spiritual Longing in C. S. Lewis*. Reprint. Grand Rapids: Eerdmans, 1999.

Cording, Ruth James. *C. S. Lewis: A Celebration of His Early Life*. Nashville: Broadman & Holman, 2000.

Dorsett, Lyle W. *A Love Observed*. Wheaton: Harold Shaw, 1998.

———. *Seeking the Secret Place*. Grand Rapids: Brazos Press, 2004.

Dorsett, Lyle W., and Marjorie Lamp Mead, eds. *C. S. Lewis Letters to Children*. New York: Collins, 1985.

Downing, David. *Into the Region of Awe: Mysticism in C. S. Lewis*. Downers Grove: InterVarsity Press, 2005.

———. *Into the Wardrobe: C. S. Lewis and the Narnia Chronicles*. San Francisco: Jossey-Bass, 2005.

———. *The Most Reluctant Convert*. Downers Grove: InterVarsity, 2002.

Duriez, Colin. *The C. S. Lewis Encyclopedia*. Wheaton: Crossway, 1990.

———. *A Field Guide to Narnia*. Downers Grove: InterVarsity, 2004.

———. *Tolkien and C. S. Lewis: The Gift of Friendship*. New York: Paulist Press, 2003.

Duriez, Colin, and David Porter. *The Inklings Handbook*. St. Louis: Chalice Press, 2001.

Edwards, Bruce L. *Not a Tame Lion*. Wheaton: Tyndale Publishers, 2005.

———. ed. *The Taste of the Pineapple: Essays on C. S. Lewis as Reader, Critic, and Imaginative Writer*. Bowling Green: Popular Press, 1988.

Ford, Paul F. *Companion to Narnia*. New York: HarperCollins, 1993.

Graham, David, ed. *We Remember C. S. Lewis: Essays and Memoirs*. Nashville: Broadman & Holman, 2001.

Green, Roger Lancelyn, and Walter Hooper. *C. S. Lewis: A Biography*. Revised Ed. New York: Harvest, 1994.

Gresham, Douglas. *Jack's Life: The Life Story of C. S. Lewis*. Nashville: Broadman & Holman, 2005.

Hinten, Marvin. *The Keys to the Chronicles*. Nashville: Broadman & Holman, 2005.

Hooper, Walter. *C. S. Lewis: A Companion and Guide*. New York: HarperCollins, 1996.

―――. *Past Watchful Dragons*. New York: Collier, 1979.

King, Don. *C. S. Lewis, Poet: The Legacy of His Poetic Impulse*. Kent: Kent State University Press, 2001.

Kreeft, Peter. *C. S. Lewis for the Third Millennium: Six Essays on the Abolition of Man*. San Francisco: Ignatius, 1994.

―――. *Everything You Always Wanted to Know about Heaven but Were Afraid to Ask*. San Francisco: Ignatius, 1990.

―――. *The Shadow-Lands of C. S. Lewis: The Man behind the Movie*. San Francisco: Ignatius, 1994.

Lewis, C. S. *An Experiment in Criticism*. Cambridge: Cambridge University Press, 1961.

―――. *Boxen: The Imaginary World of the Young C. S. Lewis*. Walter Hooper, ed. New York: Harcourt, 1986.

―――. *Mere Christianity*. New York: Touchstone Books, 1996.

―――. *On Stories*. Walter Hooper, ed. San Diego: Harvest Books, 1982.

―――. *Studies in Medieval and Renaissance Literature*. Walter Hooper, ed. Cambridge: Cambridge University Press, 1966.

―――. *Surprised by Joy*. New York: Harcourt, 1955.

Lindskoog, Kay. *Journey to Narnia*. Pasadena: Hope Publishing, 1998.

―――. *The Lion of Judah in Never-Never Land*. Grand Rapids: Eerdmans, 1973.

Manlove, Colin. *The Chronicles of Narnia: The Patterning of a Fantastic World*. Boston: Twayne, 1993.

Markos, Louis. *Lewis Agonistes: How C. S. Lewis Can Train Us to Wrestle with the Modern and Postmodern World.* Nashville: Broadman & Holman, 2003.

Martin, Thomas L., ed. *Reading the Classics with C. S. Lewis.* Grand Rapids: Baker Books, 2000.

Martindale, Wayne. *Beyond the Shadowlands: C. S. Lewis on Heaven and Hell.* Wheaton: Crossway, 2005.

Mills, David, ed. *The Pilgrim's Guide: C. S. Lewis and the Art of Witness.* Grand Rapids: Eerdmans, 1998.

Root, Jerry. "C. S. Lewis and the Problem of Evil" in *C. S. Lewis: Lightbearer in the Shadowlands: The Evangelistic Vision of C. S. Lewis.* Angus Menuge, ed. Wheaton: Crossway, 1997.

——. *The Quotable C. S. Lewis.* With Wayne Martindale. Wheaton: Tyndale House, 1990.

Sayer, George A. *Jack: A Life of C. S. Lewis.* Revised ed. Wheaton: Crossway Books, 1994.

Schakel, Peter. *Imagination and the Arts in C. S. Lewis: Journeying to Narnia and Other Worlds.* Columbia: University of Missouri Press, 2002.

——, ed. *The Longing for a Form: Essays on the Fiction of C. S. Lewis.* Kent: Kent State University Press, 1977.

——. *Reading with the Heart.* Grand Rapids: Eerdmans, 1979.

Schultz, Jeffrey D., and John West. *The C. S. Lewis Readers' Encyclopedia.* Grand Rapids: Zondervan, 1998.

Williams, Don. *Mere Humanity: G. K. Chesterton, C. S. Lewis, and J. R. R. Tolkien on the Human Condition.* Nashville: Broadman & Holman, 2005.

Study Questions

These questions are designed to help guide your enjoyment in discussing sections of *The Lion, the Witch and the Wardrobe* in classrooms and small groups. They are meant to generate dialogue and not merely to settle points of disagreement in interpretation; indeed, there may be many different answers to these questions, depending on personal life circumstances, wide or limited reading, and experience in the Christian faith. All these variables provide a good mix to ensure a rich exploration of these multilayered tales.

Finding What You're Not Looking For

THE LION, THE WITCH AND THE WARDROBE, CHAPTERS 1–3

1. What are the circumstances that cause the Pevensie children to end up in Professor Kirke's household? What is their initial reaction to being so far from home and their parents?

2. Think about the setting as you encounter Narnia for the first time. Who is in control in Narnia when Lucy first visits through the wardrobe? Why is it "always winter and never Christmas"? How is this symbolic of what is happening to the creatures who inhabit Narnia?

3. Why is Edmund so much different from his brother and sister? How would you describe his character?

4. Why are the children referred to as the "sons of Adam and daughters of Eve" by the inhabitants of Narnia? How does this factor into their personal peril and their role in saving Narnia?

Turkish Delights and Other Tempting Confections

THE LION, THE WITCH AND THE WARDROBE, CHAPTERS 4–6

1. What is the power of Turkish delight in Edmund's life? How does it captivate and enslave him? What is the Turkish delight in your life?

2. How would you describe the white witch? What kind of power does she yield? Why would Edmund, or anyone, fall prey to her cunning and sorcery?

3. When Peter and Susan bring Lucy's "odd behavior" to Professor Kirke, how does he respond? What are the professor's three options for explaining Lucy's behavior, and how does he lead Peter and Susan to the "logical" conclusion? What does he seem to think about their schooling?

4. Once in Narnia, how do the Pevensies find their bearings and learn whom to trust?

Hospitality Is as Hospitality Does

THE LION, THE WITCH AND THE WARDROBE, CHAPTERS 7–9

1. What's the difference between the ways the Beavers receive the sons and daughters of Adam and Eve and the way the witch receives them?

2. What kinds of characteristics are attributed to Aslan by Mr. and Mrs. Beaver before he arrives on the scene in person? What anticipation do these descriptions create in the children? When he does arrive, what effect does his presence have?

3. Reflect especially on Mr. Beaver's comment that Aslan "is not safe, but he is good." What are the implications of this for the children and their evolving knowledge of what to expect in Narnia? What expectations does it create for you?

4. Think about the respective character development of Lucy and Edmund. Compare and contrast the differing reactions Edmund and Lucy have in their first trip into Narnia. How do you account for their different allegiances and behaviors?

Aslan on the Move

THE LION, THE WITCH AND THE WARDROBE, CHAPTERS 10–13

1. What is Father Christmas doing in Narnia? How does his coming affect the children and the other Narnians he greets?

2. How does the coming of Aslan affect Narnia itself, its landscapes and its inhabitants? Why is this ominous to the witch? How do you react to Aslan?

3. Imagine that you are each of the four Pevensie children. What would their journals look like after their first few hours in Narnia? Write several entries on behalf of each of the children, and explain how, with each unfolding episode, they would react.

4. How does Aslan prepare them for what must be done?

Deep Magic Is Never Enough

THE LION, THE WITCH AND THE WARDROBE, CHAPTERS 14–17

1. To justify her planned execution of Edmund, the white witch cites the "Deep Magic from the Dawn of Time." What is the nature of this "Deep Magic"?

2. Why is Aslan bound to obey the dictates of the "Deep Magic"? Why does he rebuke Susan for suggesting that he might find a way around them?

3. Explain in your own words what the "Deeper Magic from Before the Dawn of Time" is, and its thematic parallel to the story of Christ in the Gospels.

4. We know there are some obvious Christian parallels in *The Lion, the Witch and Wardrobe*, including Aslan's sacrificial death on behalf of Edmund and his resurrection from the dead. What are some other parallels at work in this first Chronicle?

5. Does the end of the story make you sad or glad? What makes it easy or difficult to take the journey to Narnia? After you have been there, is there a temptation to stay, or do you want to come back and share your experiences? Keeping in mind what the professor says at the end, with whom can you entrust these experiences?

Endnotes

PREFACE

1. Lyle W. Dorsett and Marjorie Lamp Mead, eds., *C. S. Lewis Letters to Children*, (New York: Collins, 1985), 68–69.

2. C. S. Lewis, *Studies in Medieval and Renaissance Literature*, Walter Hooper, ed. (Cambridge: Cambridge University Press, 1966), 2–3.

3. Lewis explores and illustrates what he means by "looking at" and "looking along" in an intriguing essay entitled "Meditation in a Toolshed," found in *God in the Dock*, Walter Hooper, ed. (Grand Rapids: Eerdmans, 1970), 212–15.

CHAPTER 1, MEETING C. S. LEWIS: RETELLING THE GOSPEL AS A FAIRY TALE

1. For those who wish a fuller treatment of Lewis's life and times, more than we can explore here, I recommend: George Sayer, *Jack: A Life of C. S. Lewis,* revised ed. (Wheaton: Crossway, 1994); or Roger Lancelyn Green and Walter Hooper, *C. S. Lewis: A Biography,* revised ed. (New York: Harvest, 1994).

2. C. S. Lewis, *Letters to Malcolm* (New York: Harcourt, 1963), 91.

3. To learn more of the historical context surrounding Lewis's youth and his later conversion, readers should consult David Downing's exemplary study, *The Most Reluctant Convert* (Downers Grove: InterVarsity Press, 2002).

4. C. S. Lewis, *Mere Christianity,* reprint ed. (New York: Simon & Schuster, 1996), 121.

5. *Surprised by Joy* (New York: Harcourt, 1955), 179–81.

6. Ibid, 191.

7. *C. S. Lewis Letters to Children*, 95.

8. C. S. Lewis, "It All Began with a Picture," *On Stories*, Walter Hooper, ed. (New York: Harcourt, 1982), 53.

9. Readers interested in learning more about Lewis's friendship with Tolkien should consult Colin Duriez, *Tolkien and C. S. Lewis: The Gift of Friendship* (New York: Paulist Press, 2003).

10. Walter Hooper, ed. *The Letters of C. S. Lewis to Arthur Greeves* (18 October 1931) (New York: HarperCollins, 1979), 427–28.

11. Consider Tolkien's own footnote within the original publication of this essay: "The gospels are not artistic in themselves; the Art is here in the story itself, not in the telling. For the Author of the story was not the

evangelist. 'Even the world itself could not contain the books that should be written,' if that story had been fully written down."

12. "On Fairy-Stories," *Essays Presented to Charles Williams,* C. S. Lewis, ed. (Oxford: Oxford University Press, 1947), 83–84.

13. "Myth Become Fact," *God in the Dock,* Walter Hooper, ed. (Grand Rapids: Eerdmans, 1967), 66–67.

14. C. S. Lewis, *On Stories,* Walter Hooper, ed. (New York: Harcourt, 1982), 81–82.

15. Ibid, 47.

CHAPTER 2, FINDING WHAT YOU'RE NOT LOOKING FOR: *THE LION, THE WITCH AND THE WARDROBE,* CHAPTERS 1–3

1. Please note: All references to and/or quotations from *The Lion, the Witch and the Wardrobe* in this work are taken from my well-worn and well-loved copy of the single-volume paperback edition first published in New York by Collier Books in 1970, an imprint of HarperCollins Publishers. Since editions abound and pagination varies per volume, any page citations are accurate only for this specific edition and thus represent only approximate placement in other editions. Relax. The chapters in *The Lion, the Witch and the Wardrobe* are short, and you're likely to find my references without too much trouble no matter which edition you have!

CHAPTER 4, HOSPITALITY IS AS HOSPITALITY DOES: *THE LION, THE WITCH AND THE WARDROBE,* CHAPTERS 7–9

1. Whoa, wait a minute! Someone did—*me.* And it's called, ahem, *Not a Tame Lion* (Wheaton: Tyndale, 2005).

2. C. S. Lewis, *The Weight of Glory and Other Addresses,* first American paperback edition (Grand Rapids: Wm. B. Eerdmans, 1965), 5.

3. David Downing has offered readers of Lewis an excellent study of how his thought fits into the "mystical" tradition in this work: *Into the Region of Awe: Mysticism in C. S. Lewis* (Downers Grove: InterVarsity Press, 2005).

CHAPTER 6, DEEP MAGIC IS NEVER ENOUGH: *THE LION, THE WITCH AND THE WARDROBE,* CHAPTERS 14–17

1. C. S. Lewis, *Mere Christianity* (New York: Touchstone Books, 1996), 120.

Index